Liberty
and
Equality

*The Hoover Institution
gratefully acknowledges
the support of*

JOANNE AND JOHAN BLOKKER

on this project.

PHILOSOPHIC REFLECTIONS ON A FREE SOCIETY

Liberty
and
Equality

Edited by
Tibor R. Machan

HOOVER INSTITUTION PRESS

Stanford University   Stanford, California

www.hoover.org

Hoover Institution Press Publication No. 498

First printing 2002
08   07   06   05   04   03   02   9   8   7   6   5   4   3   2   1

Manufactured in the United States of America
The paper used in this publication meets the minimum requirements
of American National Standard for Information Sciences—Permanence
of Paper for Printed Library Materials, ANSI Z39.48-1984. ⊗

Library of Congress Cataloging-in-Publication Data
Liberty and Equality / edited by Tibor R. Machan.
     p.   cm. (Philosophic reflections on a free society)
   Includes bibliographical references and index.
   ISBN 0-8179-2862-6 (alk. paper)
   1. Equality.   2. Liberty.   I. Machan, Tibor R.   II. Series.
JC575 .L54   2002
320.01′1—dc21   2001039785

CONTENTS

ACKNOWLEDGMENTS

ONCE AGAIN I wish to express my gratitude to the Hoover Institution on War, Revolution and Peace and its director, John Raisian, for supporting the publication of this work. Joanne and the late Johan Blokker have again given their generous support of the Hoover Institution Press series, Philosophic Reflections on a Free Society, for which I wish to express my deep gratitude. The contributing authors gave their full cooperation, patience, and conscientiousness throughout the entire publishing process. David M. Brown has helped with some editing and I wish to thank him for this. Tina Garcia's administrative assistance was very helpful and the diligent work of Pat Baker, Ann Wood, and Marshall Blanchard of the Hoover Institution Press is also much appreciated.

T.R.M.

CONTRIBUTORS

NICHOLAS CAPALDI, the McFarlin Endowed Professor of Philosophy and Research Professor of Law at the University of Tulsa and
founder and former director of Legal Studies, teaches in the depart-
ments of political science, philosophy, religion, and the law school.
His most recent book is *The Enlightenment Project in the Analytic
Conversation.*

ELLEN R. KLEIN is an associate professor of philosophy at Flagler
College in St. Augustine, Florida. She wrote *Feminism under Fire*
(Prometheus Books, 1996) and is a critic of academic feminism
who argues against feminist political philosophy, epistemology,
philosophy of science, pedagogy, and constructs of "gender" and
"date rape."

MARK LEBAR is an assistant professor of philosophy at Ohio University, where he works on moral, social, and political philosophy.

TIBOR R. MACHAN is distinguished fellow and Freedom Commu-
nications Professor of Business Ethics and Free Enterprise at the
Leatherby Center for Entrepreneurship and Business Ethics, Argy-

ros School of Business and Economics, Chapman University, and a research fellow at the Hoover Institution.

JAN NARVESON is a professor of philosophy at the University of Waterloo in Ontario, Canada. His extensive writings on moral and political philosophy include *The Libertarian Idea* (Temple University Press, 1988; to be republished, Broadview Press, 2001), *Moral Matters* (Broadview Press, 2d edition, 1999), and (with Marilyn Friedman) *Political Correctness: For and Against* (Rowman & Littlefield, 1995). He is also the editor of *Moral Issues* (Oxford University Press, 1983) and author of several hundred papers and reviews in philosophical and other journals and book.

The Errors of Egalitarianism

Tibor R. Machan

IT WOULD BE HARD to find someone who has no sympathies whatever with even the most radical version of egalitarianism. When we witness glaring discrepancies (what some call "harsh inequalities") in wealth or opportunity between people who otherwise seem alike in every important respect, we tend to find that disturbing.

The inequality seems especially harsh when those deficiently blessed are working hard, "playing by the rules," and so forth, while those more abundantly blessed seem to have acquired their plenitude by mere luck—perhaps by being born into "the right" family—not by any special exercise of prudence, wisdom, or other virtues. It seems unfair, and the intuition or commonsense impression is that, somehow, what is unfair should be made more fair.

Exactly what people mean by fairness tends to vary, however.

There is the somewhat primitive notion of fairness, according to which benefits and harms are seen to be fairly or unfairly distributed in relation to how parents tend to divide them in a household. But a family is a special context, and what fairness means in households is not morally primary; it derives from the obligation of the parent to care for all the children in that household (but not, for example, the kids down the street or in another country). If fairness as practiced in households *were* morally primary, we would be justified in demanding that parents care not only for their own children but also for all children.[1] Even in an intuitionist view of ethics, according to which our moral obligations rest on deep-seated feelings about right and wrong, this notion does not seem to hold water. And as a matter of common sense, it is clear that trying to care for millions of kids simultaneously could lead to some obvious neglect of one's own kids, an apparent lapse of fairness. Collectivized child-rearing—letting the state function as parent, as Plato proposed—would be one logical end of the line of this approach. But again, most parents would recoil at the prospect of turning their progeny over to the government altogether.

But there is also the more plausible concern with fairness that we have noted, namely, that some people are facing dire straits through no fault of their own even as others enjoy luxury, ease, and unlimited vistas through no merit of their own. Some philosophers, Kai Nielsen[2] and Ronald Dworkin[3] for instance, go so far as to argue that the foremost public priority, coming even before liberty, should be to establish a condition of equality among human beings with respect to the distribution of benefits and harms (or, in Dworkin's argument, with respect to prospects for flourishing). They hold that the duty of public authorities is not to protect the rights of the individual to liberty but to establish a condition of more or less strict equality. There is, they suggest, a basic *right to equality*.

Radical egalitarians aim to ensure, via law and public policy, that

---

1. In some normative views it is. In the People's Republic of China some years ago, during a flood, when a father rescued another child instead of his own, his sacrifice was hailed for being consistent with communist virtue.

2. Kai Nielsen, *Equality and Liberty: A Defense of Radical Egalitarianism* (Lanham, Md.: Rowman & Littlefield, 1986).

3. Ronald Dworkin, *Sovereign Virtue* (Cambridge: Harvard University Press, 2000).

we all get the same benefits in society, the same health care, the same education, the same Internet access, the same everything. Despite the claim that "equal concern does not mean that government must ensure that everyone has the same wealth, no matter what,"[4] less radical versions veer inexorably in the same direction, pulled by the logic of the position. This is especially true now that modern liberals have regained their ideological prominence in the wake of the ideological collapse of the conservatives in the U.S. Congress, not to mention in Britain and Europe generally. Conservative politicians in particular have lost all credibility as principled defenders of small government and individual liberty, making the job of the disloyal opposition easier.[5]

Dworkin's approach is of special interest here because he claims to hold a position many contemporary defenders of the market (outside of politics) also embrace: ethical individualism. At first glance, his account is not very different from what I call classical individualism:[6] he believes "that it is objectively important that any human life, once begun, succeed rather than fail—that the potential of that life be realized rather than wasted—and that this is equally objectively important in the case of each human life."[7] Perhaps surprisingly, Dworkin also believes that "one person—the person

4. Ibid., p. 2.

5. It is not possible to defend the free system against incursions of egalitarian regimentation as a matter of principle when other types of regimentation are championed. Conservatives, for example, want subsidies and protectionist measures for business, or restrictions on personal conduct such as gambling and drug abuse. Once these exceptions to individual liberty are granted, the plea for yet other exceptions cannot be resisted as a matter of principle. This is becoming evident even vis-à-vis freedom of speech, as both liberals and conservatives make allowances for limiting it, whether to protect flags or political correctness.

6. Tibor R. Machan, *Classical Individualism: The Supreme Importance of Each Human Being* (London: Routledge, 1998). See also David L. Norton, *Personal Destinies: A Philosophy of Ethical Individualism* (Princeton: Princeton University Press, 1976) and, more radically, Ayn Rand, *The Virtue of Selfishness: A New Concept of Egoism* (New York: New American Library, 1961).

7. Dworkin, *Sovereign Virtue*, p. 448.

whose life it is—has a special responsibility for each life, and that in virtue of that special responsibility he or she has a right to make the fundamental decisions that define, for him, what a successful life would be."[8]

This kind of fundamental regard for personal autonomy would seem to be sharply at odds with coercive egalitarianism. But Dworkin goes on to claim that "in constructing a theory of political morality," we will indeed arrive at "an egalitarian theory, because [public morality] will insist that government must treat the life of each person it governs as having great and equal importance, and construct its economic and other structures and policies with that egalitarian principle in mind."[9]

But Dworkin makes an invalid jump here—from what individuals are responsible for, to what *governments* are responsible for. And his claim is self-contradictory. If we accept that governments must engage in the equalizing process claimed to be their function, they will end up squelching the individual autonomy the ultimate value of which is said to justify egalitarian rule in the first place. If every time an individual achieves something beyond what has been accomplished by others, one must give it up—no matter how personally valuable to oneself—then that person will hardly be responsible *in fact* for making a success of his or her own life, of developing his or her potentials wisely or managing assets prudently. One will have less of a chance than one would under freedom either to excel or fail at what is, by Dworkin's own characterization, a personal moral project, one that in Robert Nozick's phrase requires "moral space" and thus may not be constricted by government and other uninvited agents.[10] Instead one will be thwarted and undermined at

8. Ibid., p. 449.
9. Ibid.
10. Robert Nozick, *Anarchy, State, and Utopia* (New York: Basic Books, 1974), p. 57. It is not clear that Dworkin grasps the legal preconditions for exercising personal responsibility. He does not discuss free will, but his discussion of

every turn. Dworkin ignores the fact that (adult) personal success is self-initiated, self-guided, and self-experienced. It simply cannot be divinely distributed and mandated by a governmental central planner.

Apart from the paradox in Dworkin's stance, is there any merit to the egalitarian thesis?[11] Is it in any basic respect superior to the idea it opposes, to wit, that the first duty of a community's legal authorities is "to secure these rights," rights "to life, liberty, and the pursuit of happiness"?

The contributors to this volume deal with many of the questions that arise in considerable detail. Here I can give only a few hints of certain fundamental philosophical difficulties with the egalitarian stance.

There is the problem, for example, that to bring about the requisite equality there must be a group of persons quite unequal to everyone else in their power to impose their will! ("All animals are equal, but some are more equal than others.") Even if the process begins democratically, the delegation of the kind of power needed to establish strong equality would rapidly render the administrators of public affairs significantly unequal in their power over others. The master and the servant do not enjoy the same level of control over each other.

When John Rawls argues that we need equal distribution of wealth, except when unequal distribution is to everyone's benefit, the policies designed to achieve this goal will have to be imposed

---

ethical individualism suggests that he holds the view that morality requires it. After all, how else could one be personally responsible? In Rawls, however, we do see a direct smack at free will, one that renders his support of egalitarianism more coherent than Dworkin's. See John Rawls, *A Theory of Justice* (Cambridge: Harvard University Press, 1971), p. 104.

11. The claim that the capitalism or quasi capitalism of the past engendered the phenomenon of the rich getting richer while the poor get poorer is strongly disputed in Robert W. Fogel, *The Fourth Great Awakening and the Future of Egalitarianism* (Chicago: University of Chicago Press, 1999).

by people whose power to bring it about (or even to make the determination about what is the "best" mix of equality and inequality) puts them on a different playing field from the rest of us. On the other hand, if in keeping with the egalitarian ideal no one is allowed more power over others than anybody else, then what we have is a free society, in which inequalities of various kinds will pile up willy-nilly anyway, as they always do when a human society is free. And this points up a certain incoherence in the egalitarian ideal, suggesting that it is unworkable from the get-go.

There are problems with the assumptions underlying egalitarianism as well. As developed by Rawls, for example, the theory claims that everyone is ultimately in the same boat, morally speaking. None of us, for example, morally deserves any special advantages. This is because our character depends "in large part on fortunate family and social circumstances for which [one] can claim no credit."[12]

In this view, none of us has very much to do with how we turn out, for better or for worse. When some of us end up better situated than others, this can have nothing to do with personal effort and achievement, only with luck. Nor is anybody responsible for failures, or for acting as a predator or oppressor of others. We are, morally speaking, all the same, neither better nor worse, neither more nor less deserving of the advantages we enjoy in life. All merely happens as it must. And since we are all in the same boat, a

---

12. Rawls, *A Theory of Justice*, p. 104. It is interesting that Rawls draws much of his ammunition here from someone who, in opposition to him, supported laissez-faire, namely, Frank Knight, *Selected Essays* (Chicago: University of Chicago Press, 1999). Rawls credits Knight in his book (p. 311) but does not heed Knight's concern about empowering the state to remedy the unfairness. I would, however, dispute that there is anything at all unfair in someone's possession of undeserved assets. So long as these assets were not stolen or otherwise unjustly obtained—and one certainly cannot argue that the beauty of a supermodel or height of a champion basketball player are so obtained—there is nothing morally objectionable afoot here. Moral wrongs have to do with choices, not genetic inheritance.

team, we are committed to sharing our benefits and burdens. Again, of course, some are more equal than others when it comes to actually organizing society along alleged egalitarian lines. Furthermore, those who accept the Rawlsian viewpoint would, one may assume, be regarded as morally more astute, even more worthwhile, than those who reject it, so much so that the former would be justified in coercing the latter into compliance with the social organization Rawls would like to set up.

The picture Rawls paints of our moral equality, if true, does suggest that there is something very wrong with the wide discrepancies of advantages in people's lives. If it just happens to happen, through no one's fault or credit at all, that a great many people are struggling to get by while a select few like Bill Gates are inordinately well off, that would certainly be morally problematic. Although such a purely accidental allotment of triumphs and tribulations could not by itself justify attempts to flatten the status quo, it would be the beginning of the case for such reform. If, in addition, we are all on same team, belonging together, all equally responsible for each other, this moral duty, combined with the first condition, might justify mandatory sharing of the team's benefits and burdens.[13]

Philosophers Peter Unger and Peter Singer call for just such reform in their books *Living High and Letting Die: Our Illusion of Innocence*[14] and *Practical Ethics*.[15] As Unger puts it, "On pain of living

13. I discuss the sort of moral issue involved here in Tibor R. Machan, *Generosity: Virtue in Civil Society* (Washington, D.C.: Cato Institute, 1998). Suffice it to say that whatever moral responsibilities to help those in need we may have, we may not be coerced into fulfilling them unless a prior commitment is involved, as when parents are obliged to help their children, or an insurance firm is obliged to help its clients in event of a disaster covered under its policy.

14. Peter Unger, *Living High and Letting Die: Our Illusion of Innocence* (New York: Oxford University Press, 1996).

15. Peter Singer, *Practical Ethics* (Cambridge: Cambridge University Press, 1993).

a life that's seriously immoral, a typical well-off person, like you and me, must give away most of her financially valuable assets, and much of her income, directing the funds to lessen efficiently the serious suffering of others."

Unger's claim isn't merely a lament. Nor is it merely a call for some measure of generosity, either local or global. It is, rather, a demand for the coercive redistribution of wealth. Yet it is also a call for personal conduct that is supposedly consistent with morality or ethics. Under the Ungerian ethic, all of us should work for drastic reforms in the political systems in which Westerners happen to live with all the wealth they happen to have. Egalitarianism is thus both a political and a moral crusade, demanding that people do the right thing via their political institutions and, when it comes to their personal conduct, demanding that they give away all of their own wealth beyond whatever is deemed subsistence level.

Yet the call for the mandatory redistribution of benefits and harms via public policy, and the imperative to exercise personal generosity and charity, go contrary to the original Rawlsian assumption that none of us can help what we are and do, and can be assigned no credit or blame for what we have done or not done.[16] And therein lies the rub: no one can agree to support egalitarian public policy or personal morality if no one has any control over his or her own conduct.

To say, "One *ought to* establish public policies that equalize economic and other relevant conditions among people throughout the world" is to implore people *to do something they may or may not choose to do*. It assumes that they are able to choose what they will think, how they will act. It assumes *moral self-responsibility*. Yet moral responsibility cannot be attributed if Rawls is right and our moral

16. Tom Palmer suggested to me that Rawls's narrow type of moralism is a uniquely Kantian sort in which, although no one deserves any benefits from virtuous conduct, one can achieve higher moral status via holding the right convictions about justice and fairness—salvation by grace rather than acts.

character is not of our own making but is merely a predetermined epiphenomenon of "family and social circumstances for which [one] can claim no credit" nor blame. *Que sera, sera*, all the way down, as it were.

But if we do have the chance to make moral choices in our lives, then at least the Rawlsian egalitarian project is incoherent. Because then not all of us who find ourselves in dire straits absolutely had to be. And some are there through no fault of their own but through the clear fault of others, who are then morally responsible themselves.[17]

Nor need all those with greater advantages have failed to deserve them.[18] It is not only luck that led to Bill Gates being a billionaire while many others were barely getting by from month to month, with little to set aside for rainy days. Bill Gates may have been born with talents or potentials that others were not born with, but he then had to choose to diligently exercise and develop that capacity. Our fate does have something to do with our choices, even if our choices are not *all* that matter.[19] And if one cannot reap the fruits of those choices, there is serious injustice afoot in the society. If

17. For more on this, see Tibor R. Machan, *Initiative: Human Agency and Society* (Stanford, Calif.: Hoover Institution Press, 2000).

18. For a challenging discussion of the alleged connection between desert and justice, see Gillian Brock, "Just Deserts and Needs," *Southern Journal of Philosophy* 37 (1999): 165–88. It should be noted, though, that not all defenders of justice as consisting primarily of respect for and protection of individual rights to life, liberty, and property rest on the belief that one deserves one's belongings. No one can argue that someone deserves both eyes or two kidneys, yet it does not follow at all that one has no right to these and others need not respect, nor may one protect this right. One can well argue that no one deserves to have one's eyes plucked out.

19. Here it may be worth noting that quite apart from any achievement or failure related to economic well-being, there can be many people for whom a modest economic prosperity is all they may require to flourish in life. One size does not fit all; some create wealth, some art, some philosophy, and many are willing to live with what they they are able to get through these endeavors.

morality is to make sense at all, then we are *not* all in the same boat as far as our achievements or failures are concerned.

Now if that is so, an egalitarian regime would run counter to justice by running counter to these choices. It would also unjustly exculpate oppressors everywhere who, for sure, did not have to impose their tyrannical measures on others and thereby produce the dire straits that tyranny tends to produce. All those famines in countries where productivity is thwarted by regimes that pillage wealth instead of making it possible for people to keep what they produce (like Ethiopia and its neighbors) cannot be prevented by redistributing wealth. It is precisely such redistribution and pillaging that kills the goose that lays the golden egg, stifling productivity by unjustly depriving people of the fruits of their work, ingenuity, and, yes, even luck. Famines must be fought through investment, long-term planning, and, most of all, the establishment of private property rights that allow people to invest and plan.

Indeed, if wealth were completely equally divided throughout the world, this division would result in everyone's having extremely little so that hardly any projects costing considerable sums could be supported. One advantage of the wealthy to the poor is that the wealthy can invest in costly enterprises that the poor can use, at least now and then. It is an odd kind of universal humanitarianism that must lay waste to all human endeavor. But such is the only possible end game of an adamantly egalitarian public policy.

Another basic flaw in the Rawlsian framework is the assumption that if no one deserves advantages in life, it follows that others are authorized to redistribute the total sum of advantages according to a scheme of fairness. That is a non sequitur. Where does this authority come from, given that it involves subjecting millions of persons to measures they may well not have accepted on their own?

In any case, throughout nature, including human social life, ranking is unavoidable.[20] Differences emerge, persist, and have an impact. No matter how much one might wish for a different kind of universe, there will always be better and worse cases of human conduct, institutions, products, and so on. It is telling that not even those who preach full egalitarianism can stick to their principles.

As an example, consider that famous liberal institution, National Public Radio. The sheer limitation of time requires selectivity. NPR's bleeding-heart egalitarianism is also belied by a certain saturating elitism. The same is true of academic moral philosophy, which is dominated by egalitarian sentiments and ideas; in practice, however, academic moral philosophers are picky about whom they will admit into their ranks. Such academic stars as John Rawls and Peter Singer are all happily housed in highly ranked institutions, despite their self-proclaimed egalitarianism. And if they were not there, others would be.

Consider also that even noncommercial organizations select artists on the basis of some standard, a standard of quality and content that must include some performers and exclude others. My local noncommercial jazz and blues station constantly features favorites and highlights public performances of the more renowned artists, blatantly discriminating against the less capable and successful. Joe Lunchbucket riffing in his garage never gets the same kind of promotion, even if his display is open to the public.

The kind of impossible egalitarianism preached by socialists and other sentimentalists is not an option. All we can aspire to do is

---

20. For a satirical depiction of what extreme egalitarianism would look like, see Kurt Vonnegut Jr., "Harrison Bergeron," *The Magazine of Fantasy and Science Fiction* (October 1961). "The year was 2081, and everybody was finally equal. They weren't only equal before God and the law. They were equal every which way. Nobody was smarter than anybody else. Nobody was better looking than anybody else. Nobody was stronger or quicker than anybody else. All this equality was due to the 211th, 212th, and 213th Amendments to the Constitution, and to the unceasing vigilance of agents of the United States Handicapper General."

rank on the basis of valid standards, ones that may be difficult to identify but that we are nonetheless responsible for discovering and applying. Most of nature is differentiated mainly by reference to power or fitness for physical survival. But human beings have the power to choose how we approach the ranking that is inherent in all of nature. In human affairs, such ranking needs to be rationally justified, based on merit, and carried out with justice and with respect for basic rights.

The Declaration of Independence tells us that that "all men are created equal." Ever since, critics of the idea of the free society have argued that this is nonsense because, in fact, we are quite evidently not all created equal. Indeed, they stress, the truth is we ought to be equal—it is only fair and just—but we are not. Nature bungled. Accordingly, force should be deployed in society not primarily to combat criminal conduct but to make us all equal in all important respects.

Of course, the Declaration was referring to equality of rights, equality of legal status in society. Men are said to be "created equal" in the respect of possessing unalienable rights to, among other conditions, "life, liberty, and the pursuit of happiness." In other words, we are all rights possessors. That does not mean we are—or should be—equal in our height, fortune, intelligence, looks, or talents.

The point of the Declaration's limited egalitarianism—if we want to characterize it in such terms—is to stress a distinctive requirement of organized social life. Despite all the clear and undeniable differences among human beings, there are some basic principles we ought to respect and protect, namely, our fundamental rights as agents of our choices. Any kind of broader egalitarianism is both impossible and, to the extent that its incoherent program is coercively imposed, blatantly unjust.

That is not, however, how many famous thinkers approach the matter. Consider the late Isaiah Berlin, who said that "the assumption is that equality needs no reasons, only inequality does so. . . .

If I have a cake and there are ten persons among whom I wish to divide it, then if I give exactly one tenth to each, this will not, at any rate automatically, call for justification: whereas if I depart from this principle of equal division I am expected to produce a special reason."[21] This same notion is developed in great detail by Dworkin.

Yet the case for full equality does not prove what it tries to prove. Berlin's remark, for example, only shows what is expected of one who sets out to divide things within a group, as when parents distribute benefits among children, coaches among teammates, and so forth. But again, as when the moral obligations within a family are taken as applying to all situations whatever, a particular circumstance is here being universalized without warrant. After all, there are many occasions when *unequal* distribution is accepted as self-evidently appropriate. Why not pick one of those as the standard and model of social organization? For example, if one gives Christmas gifts and does so quite unequally, depending on how close one is to the recipient, that is taken for granted as normal.

But more fundamental than either equality or inequality as such is the nature of human beings as rational animals and, given that nature, the rightness of being able to choose one's own path, voluntarily. The fact that all human beings possess rights to life, liberty, and the pursuit of happiness equally depends first on recognizing how and why any given individual, in respect of his or her human characteristics, could possess such a right. Then it becomes clear that other individuals possessing the same characteristics must also have rights of the same general kind.

Most of these remarks bear on the moral status of equality and pay little heed to the practical prospects of securing it. We have noted, though, that Rawls is aware of some of the adverse results

21. Isaiah Berlin, "Equality," *Proceedings of the Aristotelian Society* 56 (1955–1956): 132.

of such a policy since he exempts inequalities that will produce benefits all around. As the saying goes, a rising tide lifts all boats, large, medium, or small. And it seems clear, even to Rawls, that unequal distribution of resources, initial or otherwise, tends to engender productivity, mainly by virtue of leaving incentives in place that are undoubtedly contrary to egalitarian principles.[22]

Although this is not a decisive reason to forgo attempts to secure economic and other equality, it does suggest the problem with attempting to do so. It also suggests a main reason why egalitarianism is morally troublesome: it fails to come to terms with the fact that not all inequalities among human beings are accidental, a matter merely of bad luck. People also often *become* or *remain* unequal, in virtue of acting in laudable or not-so-laudable ways, of their own volition. They do not just happen to turn out that way. And to attempt to ram everyone into the same procrustean bed would not only be destructive of the general welfare but also cripple the ability to choose morally.

22. For a clear indication of this, see James L. Payne, *Costly Returns, Burdens of the US Tax System* (San Francisco: ICS Press, 1993).

CHAPTER ONE

The Meaning
of Equality

Nicholas Capaldi

EQUALITY IS BOTH a descriptive concept and a normative concept. As a descriptive concept, equality is, by definition, an adjectival relation between entities that are identical in some specific respect. No two entities can be identical in all respects, for then they would not be two entities but the same entity. The equality may be one of quantity or quality. Equality may be predicated of things, persons, or social entities such as institutions, groups, and so on.

Equality is also a normative concept. As a normative concept, equality is the notion that there is some special respect in which all human beings are in fact equal (descriptive) but that this factual equality requires that we treat them in a special way. Special treatment may mean ensuring identical treatment, or it may mean differential treatment to restore them to or to aid them in reaching or realizing the specific factual state.

Equality as a normative concept, as we shall soon show, is central to modern political and social debate. All disagreements about equality as a normative concept center on (1) factual claims about the specific sense or senses in which human beings are identical, (2) what constitutes relevant special treatment, that is, which specific senses carry normative weight, and (3) factual claims about which public policies are consistent and coherent with and effective in ensuring the relevant special treatment.

The ancients held to an organic and hierarchical conception of the world, one, therefore, that was antiegalitarian. All of nature, including the social world, consists of a series of interlocking entities, each with its own built-in goal. Each entity in turn was a means to the satisfaction of a higher-level goal. The social world was highly stratified to reflect differences of ability that in turn led to differences of function and a corresponding difference in status. The ancient world thus held to the notion of a collective good, that is, a good that was more important than and subsumed all of the lesser goods. This view was reflected in actual social practice, so that even within Athenian democracy, women, slaves, and aliens were excluded from citizenship. The collective good consisted of the survival of the city as an internally self-ruled entity. It was the city, or polis, that was the locus of freedom, understood as self-rule. Freedom was not predicated on individuals. Rather, individuals were fulfilled when they performed their relevant proper function in maintaining the city's freedom. No sharp distinction was made among politics, ethics, and religion. Ultimate fulfillment came within the political order.

Classical political theorists advanced the same view. In Plato's *Republic,* a just society was identified with a harmonious society, and a harmonious society consisted of one in which the division of labor was exactly correlated with individual differences of ability. Even when Plato seemingly recognized superior women and advocated the equality of women, many scholars have maintained that he did so tongue-in-cheek and ultimately stressed the need for an overriding functional division of labor. For Aristotle, equality meant the "same treatment of similar persons,"[1] that is, persons who had the same status. Aristotle was more concerned that those who were unequal be treated differently. Moreover, the demand for equality on the part of those who are unequal or inferior leads, according to Aristotle, to revolution.[2] Among Roman thinkers, the Stoics asserted a form of factual equality in that all men possessed the rational capacity to grasp the universal order, but the Stoics did not draw from this any normative conclusions about altering social status.

MEDIEVAL WORLD

Christianity is the origin of the modern conception of equality, but, as we shall see, its full impact does not come into play until the Reformation. Christianity proclaimed the equal moral worth of all persons in the eyes of God. Equality is now understood as intrinsic to the human condition. It is the special respect in which all human beings are in fact equal (descriptive).

Christians drew both on Stoic doctrine and the Hebrew notion from Genesis that all human beings "male and female" were created in the "image of God." The Christian doctrine of equality as expressed by Paul (Galatians 3:26–29) is that "There is neither Jew nor Greek, there is neither bond nor free, there is neither male nor female: for ye are all one in Christ Jesus." This view was repeated in Colossians 3:10–11. There are echoes of this conception of equality in Confucianism, Hinduism, and Islam.

The question arises as to what specific normative implications follow from this conception of equality in the medieval Christian context. Recognizing equality among human beings requires that

---

1. Aristotle, *Politics*, translated by Benjamin Jowett, in *Britannica Great Books*, vol. 9 (Chicago: 1952), VII, 14.
2. Ibid., VI, 1.

we treat them in a special way. Special treatment may mean ensuring identical treatment, or it may mean differential treatment to restore them to or to aid them in reaching the specific factual state.

To understand how this developed in the medieval Christian context, we need to recognize the political innovation of Christianity. In the words of Eric Voegelin, Christianity dedivinized the state. That is, Christians denied that ultimate human fulfillment was to be achieved through participation in the polis. A distinction is introduced between politics on the one side and religion and ethics on the other. Fulfillment comes though participation in the Church. Christians, then, occupy two "cities," to use Augustine's conception. Whereas the role of the polis in Aristotle was a positive one, namely, to help make human beings good or to achieve fulfillment, the role of the state in Augustine's scheme is negative, namely, to thwart evil, or what we would call maintain law and order. Christian liberty consists in the recognition by the state of the independent status of the Church, and that fulfillment comes within the spiritual domain. This is the origin of the modern conception of limiting the power of the state.

Because fulfillment comes by participation within the Church, Christians have no direct interest in political participation or political rights such as equality before the law. Christians could technically even be slaves. Slavery was held to be a consequence of sin. With regard to membership within the Church, Christians still maintained the classical hierarchical conception. Clergy were distinguished from laypeople. This was not considered a violation of the notion of Christian equality because to achieve salvation, the sacraments needed to be administered by someone in a theologically superior position. Christians were all equally entitled to the special treatment of receiving the sacraments that paved the way to eternal salvation in the next life. Non-Christians were all equally entitled to become Christians and subsequently to receive the sacraments. They were not all equally entitled to administer the sacraments. Moreover, the sacraments could be denied to Christians who had been excommunicated precisely because they threatened the independent existence and integrity of the Church. Becket's conflict with Henry II comes to mind in this context. In short, Christian equality was seen in the medieval period to require special treatment understood in a way that led not to identical treatment but to differential treatment.

Two important consequences of Christian equality were the gradual disappearance of slavery in Europe and the fact that the Church served as the main institution of social mobility. When the issue of slavery with regard to the Native Americans in the New World was debated, it was Aristotle's argument about natural slaves that served as the basis for advocating slavery, and it was the Christian conception of the equality of all before God that served as the basis for opposing slavery. It was now thought that someone who had been baptized, including the native population of the Western Hemisphere, could not be enslaved.

REFORMATION

Equality became a central notion with the advent of modernity, specifically the Protestant Reformation. Let us begin with modernity. The difference between the classical viewpoint and the modern viewpoint is the locus of standards. For classical thinkers, including medieval thinkers, all standards whether of truth, goodness, or beauty were structural features of the world external to human beings. What gave authority to some and not to others was the belief that some individuals had direct and immediate access to those external standards (by knowledge or grace). Once those standards were apprehended, our obligation was to conform to them. The object of wisdom was conformity to the natural order of the world.

For modern thinkers, all standards are internal. The apprehension of these internal standards might lead to contact with a transcendent and/or external order (as in Descartes), but the initial apprehension was internal. The internality of standards was reflected in areas as diverse as science, where Copernicus made us aware of the relativity of perception, and art, where Renaissance artists gloried in the exploration of perspective. Moreover, the apprehension of internal standards required that we conform to them, but conformity to internal standards came to mean the transformation of the external world to conform to these internal standards. From commerce to technology to landscape gardening, modernity led to a transformation of the understanding of how individuals relate to the world.

The medieval Aristotelian synthesis in which all of nature and humanity were linked in an interlocking series of organic associations arranged in hierarchical order was rejected. Nature was not an organism but a mechanism created by God, and we as individuals replicated God's creativity by transforming the world through good works (including commerce and industry, not only charity) inspired by the internally apprehended divine vision. There was no collective good to be authoritatively apprehended in nature, only a collection of individually apprehended goods whose continuity and coherence were vouchsafed by God.

In science, in religion, in morals, and in politics, the Aristotelian hierarchical synthesis was challenged. One of the most important challenges was the rejection of the idea of natural political hierarchies, both within the Church and in the secular political sphere. The first and most striking instance was the Protestant attack on the hierarchical notion of the Church. As Luther put it in "To the Christian Nobility" (1520), "It is pure invention that popes, bishops, priests and monks are to be called the 'spiritual estate' . . . . There is really no difference . . . . it is intolerable that in the canon law so much importance is attached to the freedom, life, property of the clergy . . . . Why are your life and limb, property and honor so free, and mine not? . . . Whence comes this great distinction between those who are equally Christian? Only from human laws and inventions!"[3] Calvin expressed the full political implications of Reformation Christian equality. Authority derives from voluntary agreement among equals to submit—this is first confined to the organization of the Church and then extended to the entire political sphere. Anabaptists, most notably Thomas Münzer, went even further and asserted complete social equality to be achieved by violence if necessary. In short, modern egalitarianism originated in the Christian notion of equality as reflected within the context of other modern institutions and practices.

The so-called Protestant work ethic promoted the notion of the inner-directed individual, an emphasis on work or achievement, equality before the law and differentiation based on achievement. The insistence on equality before the law was an expression of the notion of Christian liberty. In rejecting a hierarchical conception of the world, Protestants could acquiesce in an arrangement in which the political realm was not subordinate to the religious realm. At the same time, the political realm was obliged to respect the traditional spiritual realm of Christianity. The spiritual realm was now understood in Protestant terms to mean the opportunity to do God's work by transforming the world economically and all of its attendant circumstances. Equality before the law came to mean that there should be no legal barriers to economic activity that did not apply equally to everyone. To place legal barriers to equal participation in the economic realm was to thwart God's plan.

Because not all were equal in their achievement, not all were to be treated in the same manner. There was to be a meritocracy, but the meritocracy was a reflection not of simple personal merit but of

3. Martin Luther, "To the Christian Nobility," in *Three Treatises* (1520; Reprint, Philadelphia: Muhlenberg Press 1960), pp. 14–19.

divine preordination. It was God, after all, who inspired us and accounted for the differences in achievement. However, higher status was more likely to be accompanied by a sense of greater responsibility, not by the privileges of self-indulgence.

This specifically Calvinist notion of political and legal equality influenced the Dutch, British, and American Revolutions. The Calvinist and Anabaptist influences converged in the English Civil War, specifically in a group known as the *Levellers*. The Levellers' membership reflected what we would now call the rising middle classes—small property owners, tradesmen, artisans, and apprentices. They produced a vast pamphlet literature in which, among other things, John Lilburne asserted the notion that no one has authority without consent. In a famous debate held at Putney (suburb of London) in 1647 with the officers at the Army Council meeting, speaking on behalf of the Levellers, Colonel Rainborough asserted that "the poorest he that is in England hath a life to live as the greatest he"; no one is obliged to obey a government "he hath not had a voice to put himself under."[4] An irate Ireton responded on behalf of the officers that because the poor could outvote the rich, "why may not those men vote against all property?" Hence we get the derogatory expression *Levellers*, although this was certainly a misrepresentation of their views. The Levellers, being serious Protestants, wanted to deny the franchise to all those whom they considered lacking in moral independence, such as almstakers and house servants.

A much more radical group were the so-called Diggers. Their spokesperson Gerrard Winstanley rejected private property as a reflection of original sin and claimed that "one man hath as much

---

4. Statement made at the Agreement at Putney (October 1647). Quoted in the *Encyclopaedia Britannica*, vol. 29, 15th ed. (1986), p. 62.

rights to the earth as another."[5] He attributed the existence of poverty to exploitation by the rich, and advocated a form of agrarian communism.

The difference between the Levellers and the Diggers is a significant one and heralds an ongoing dialectic in the development of modern notions of equality. We might designate this as the difference between a relative equality and an absolute equality. Relative egalitarianism is the position that some specific existing practice or institution is unjust because it fosters inequality of treatment based on irrelevant differences. Absolute egalitarianism is the advocacy of a total equality that seems to entail a collective conception of the good in which the individual good is subsumed.

What the Levellers challenged was the political power structure and not the economic and social system. Their challenge was a consistent expression both of the religious dimension of Calvinism and of the commitment to doing God's work in an increasingly market-oriented society. The Diggers, on the other hand, reflected the medieval Anabaptist call for complete equality within a feudal agrarian economy still committed to the notion of a collective good. The Levellers adhered to the Platonic-Augustinian insight that we live in two cities so that given original sin this world would always be an imperfect reflection of the City of God. Poverty was a result of a lack of moral independence that, in turn, was a result of original sin. The Diggers asserted the immanentization of the eschaton, so that not only were individuals not responsible for their own poverty but also that some sort of social utopia was possible here on earth.

Protestants during this period saw an important connection between politics and economics. The desire for political equality, that

5. Quoted from G. L. Abernethy, *The Idea of Equality: An Anthology* (Richmond, Va.: John Knox Press, 1959). (Quote originally appeared in "Truth Lifting Up Its Head Above Scandals," 1649.)

is, government by consent, did not reflect any desire to exercise power for power's sake or to remake society. On the contrary, Protestants were largely focused on protecting the private sphere and the spiritual dimension from political corruption. Rather the connection they perceived between politics and economics derived from the fact that government controlled large parts of the economy (granting privileges such as monopolies, sinecures, land grants, etc.) so that political equality led to economic equality. Economic equality meant the liberty to pursue God's work in this world, not an equal distribution of the spoils. Part of that political equality was equality before the law.

Both Hobbes and Locke articulated doctrines of natural right and social contract that reflect this Protestant framework. The modern doctrine of natural right replaced the medieval doctrine of natural law as the fundamental bulwark against political oppression. In a nonteleological universe, natural law had lost its meaning. The classical idea of law is that it is a command from an authoritative source external to humanity. The modern idea of law is that it is a directive from an authoritative source internal to humanity. The physical world of modern science is mechanistic and not teleological; natural law in the normative sense can no longer be intelligibly applied to both the human and physical world. Teleology is to be found only within the human world. This is the origin of natural rights. The starting point (ontologically, axiologically, and epistemologically) is individualism. From this individualism we deduce conclusions about the social world. In its Lockean formulation, individualism reflected a Protestant moral and religious conception of the relation between the individual and God. Each individual was alleged to have a built-in end or set of such consistent ends. In its original Lockean formulation, these ends (e.g., life, liberty, and property) were designated as *rights* (qualified as natural, human, etc.); they were teleological. Rights, so understood, were absolute, did not conflict, and were possessed only by individual human beings. Rights were morally absolute or fundamental because they were derived from human nature and God (or later the categorical imperative), and as such could not be overridden; the role of these rights was to protect the human capacity to choose. Finally, such rights imposed only duties of noninterference.

ENLIGHTENMENT AND THE FRENCH REVOLUTION

Enlightenment[6] is a term used broadly by historians of ideas to refer to the intellectual and social ferment in Western Europe during the eighteenth century. Our intention is not to generalize about this entire period but to identify a specific, salient project that we shall call the Enlightenment Project. What do we mean by the Enlightenment Project? The Enlightenment Project is the attempt to define and explain the human predicament through science as well as to achieve mastery over it through the use of a social technology. This project originated in France in the eighteenth century with the *philosophes*. The most influential among them were d'Alembert, La Mettrie, Condillac, Helvétius, d'Holbach, Turgot, Condorcet, Cabanis, and Voltaire.

Isaiah Berlin characterizes the Project as follows:

> [T]here were certain beliefs that were more or less common to the entire party of progress and civilization, and this is what makes it proper to speak of it as a single movement. These were, in effect, the conviction that the world, or nature, was a single whole, subject to a single set of laws, in principle discoverable by the intelligence of man; that the laws which governed inanimate nature were in principle the same as those which governed plants, animals and sentient beings; that man was capable of improvement; that there existed certain objectively recognizable human goals which all men,

6. Much of this discussion of the Enlightenment is taken from Nicholas Capaldi, *The Enlightenment Project in the Analytic Conversation* (Boston: Kluwer, 1998), chapter one.

rightly so described, sought after, namely, happiness, knowledge, justice, liberty, and what was somewhat vaguely described but well understood as virtue; that these goals were common to all men as such, were not unattainable, nor incompatible, and that human misery, vice and folly were mainly due to ignorance either of what these goals consisted in or of the means of attaining them—ignorance due in turn to insufficient knowledge of the laws of nature. . . . Consequently, the discovery of general laws that governed human behaviour, their clear and logical integration into scientific systems of psychology, sociology, economics, political science and the like (though they did not use these names)—and the determination of their proper place in the great corpus of knowledge that covered all discoverable facts, would, by replacing the chaotic amalgam of guesswork, tradition, superstition, prejudice, dogma, fantasy and "interested error" that hitherto did service as human knowledge and human wisdom (and of which by far the chief protector and instigator was the Church), create a new, sane, rational, happy, just and self-perpetuating human society, which, having arrived at the peak of attainable perfection, would preserve itself against all hostile influences, save perhaps those of nature."[7]

Randall identifies the intellectual origins of the project as follows: "Voltaire and his successors took over and used four main bodies of English ideas. First, there was Newtonian science, which was developed in France into a thoroughgoing materialism. Secondly, there was natural religion, or Deism, which the French pushed to atheism. Thirdly, there was Locke and British empiricism, which became theoretically a thoroughgoing sensationalism, and practically the omnipotence of the environment. Finally, there were British political institutions as interpreted by Locke, the apologist for 1688, which became the basis of the political theories of the Revolution."[8]

7. I. Berlin, *The Magus of the North: J. G. Hamann and the Origins of Modern Irrationalism* (London: John Murray, 1993), pp. 27–28.

8. J. H. Randall, *The Career of Philosophy* (New York: Columbia University Press, 1962), p. 862.

This project had three philosophical elements: metaphysical, epistemological, and axiological.

Metaphysically, the *philosophes* who formulated the Enlightenment Project were philosophic naturalists: they asserted both that the physical world was the only reality and that it could be explained exclusively by modern natural science. La Mettrie's *L'Homme machine* (1747) specifically aimed to reduce mental processes to their physiological causes. La Mettrie openly declared atheism:

> The universe will never be happy, unless it is atheistic. . . . If atheism were generally accepted, all the forms of religion would then be destroyed and cut off at the roots. . . . Deaf to all other voices, tranquil mortals would follow only the spontaneous dictates of their own being, the only commands which can never be despised with impunity and which alone can lead us to happiness. . . . Let us then conclude boldly that man is a machine, and that in the whole universe there is but a single substance differently modified."[9]

Its epistemology is Aristotle's and Locke's epistemology without a soul or an active intellect. The product of this is empiricism. Following Locke, Condillac was led to engage in analysis, the breaking down of the contents of the human mind into elementary units and then reconstituting or ordering those units into a whole. The whole was to be understood in terms of its constituent and separable parts. Departing from Locke, Condillac suggested that sensory impressions could give rise to all of our mental operations without reference to a self or active intellect. Cabanis summarizes the connection between the metaphysics and the epistemology as follows: "We are doubtless not still required to prove that physical sensibility is the source of all the ideas and of all the habits which constitute the moral existence of man: Locke, Bonnet, Condillac,

---

9. J. A. La Mettrie, *L'Homme machine*, edited by A. Vartanian (Princeton: Princeton University Press, 1960), pp. 175–76.

Helvétius have carried this truth to the last degree of demonstration."[10]

Its axiology can be characterized as natural right, without God. Morality, according to Condillac, arises as a refinement of volitional operations that originate from a combination of both internal and external physical stimuli without the interposition of an agent. Earlier, La Mettrie, in *L'Homme machine*, denied free will in favor of determinism, but he also asserted that human materialism gave rise, in a manner never explained, to an internal teleology characterized by a hierarchy of values. This internal teleology could be perfected by a kind of medical technology. In his *Discours sur le bonheur* (1750), La Mettrie described the highest good as the maximization of the pleasurable well-being of the human machine. In his 1776 publication, *Le Commerce et le gouvernement considérés relativement l'un à l'autre*, Condillac argued against mercantilism in favor of free trade and maintained that reason would discover social laws endorsing private property.

Condillac and Helvétius used the doctrine of environmental determinism to reinforce the doctrine of natural equality. Natural equality was now understood in purely secular terms so that human beings were alleged to be naturally good. These two doctrines imply a third doctrine, perfectibility. This is the scientific or social-scientific origin of equality.

The naturalistic-mechanistic worldview allows for a social technology that could in principle solve all human problems. Hence, we see the enthusiasm for mechanistic science. Mechanistic views of human nature are attractive because they are compatible with the idea that human beings are both a tabula rasa and fundamentally good. Hence, human beings could be either caused to be good, or obstacles to their natural goodness could be removed. It was no

---

10. P.J.G. Cabanis, *Rapports du physique et du moral de l'homme*, vol. 1, 2d ed. (Paris, 1805), pp. 39, 85.

accident that freedom in the modern world came to be defined, in one version, as the absence of external constraints. In an analogous way, rationality could seemingly be promoted either mechanically or by removing constraints such as the belief in religion, authority, custom, or tradition. This has the added benefit of reinforcing the progressive-scientific story by seemingly providing a naturalistic account of why it has taken so long to arrive at the truth of the Enlightenment Project.

Given the economic and social challenges of the modern world, it seemed to many of those impatient to alter the status quo that a wholesale rejection of authority, tradition, and the religious institutions that seemed to support the status quo was the quickest way to achieve reform, hence, the enthusiasm for a seemingly liberated reason. Because traditional institutions had justified themselves on the grounds that they embodied a certain wisdom about human shortcomings, mechanistic theories about the natural goodness of human nature would seem doubly attractive to critics of the status quo.

Enlightenment psychology in particular and programmatic Enlightenment social science in general were not the product of an explication of the actual empirical accomplishments of the social sciences. Rather, these were conclusions from unargued philosophical premises and a political agenda. In practice, this led to two programs: either a militant reductivism or a miraculous functional dualism. By *functional dualism* is meant the contention that physical processes at one level were perfectly coordinated with conscious processes at another level, that is, a dualism of mechanism and teleology. This dualism is "miraculous" because without some appeal to God, it is difficult to see why a deterministic system should also function coincidentally as a teleological one. Locke believed that God could make matter "think," but within the Enlightenment Project no appeal to theistic notions was permitted. So, just as the Enlightenment Project required a providential history without God, so it required a miraculous psychological dualism without God. The Enlightenment Project never succeeded in explaining, either in its epistemology or in its psychology, how the human subject could be understood without appeal to teleology of some kind and at some level.

This is important for the consideration of equality. Earlier we noted that equality was the notion that there was some special respect in which all human beings were in fact equal (descriptive); this definition of equality has normative implications. In a teleological system, all facts do carry normative weight. For example, if it is a fact that our built-in end or purpose or goal is to achieve or reach a certain condition, then it makes sense to say that we ought to act consistently with the achievement of that condition. In a mechanical or deterministic system, there are no natural goals, merely states of affairs and, in the human case, drives. It is not clear what it would mean to say that we ought to act in order to satisfy a drive. The drive operates on its own, and it is either powerful enough or "lucky" enough to prevail or it is not.

There is one unusually disturbing and perplexing axiological problem for the Enlightenment Project. That problem is the loss of the self. As we stressed in our discussion of epistemology, proponents of the Enlightenment Project denied the existence of an active intellect with special and unique functions. As we stressed in our discussion of both metaphysics and epistemology, proponents of the Enlightenment Project denied the existence of a subject that was not an object or not reducible to a collection of objects. Most especially, this amounted to the denial of the idea of the free and personally responsible individual soul that emerged out of the Greco-Roman and Judeo-Christian worldview.

The denial of the self thus serves a number of important and interrelated purposes for the Enlightenment Project. Metaphysically it reinforces the claim that the physical world is primary. In a very important sense, the entire Western intellectual tradition prior to the Enlightenment had made self-understanding primary. Coincidentally it is a further attack on the theistic contention of a unique volitional being. Epistemologically, the denial of the self reinforces the claim that knowledge is nothing but the grasping of an external structure. Failure to grasp the structure cannot be attributed to any act of the will but becomes in principle explainable in terms of further objective structures. This gives a tremendous boost to rationalist optimism. Finally, the denial of the self serves the axiological function of providing for an objective social technology that does not depend on human attitudes that are not externally manipulable. Put in other terms, intellectual virtue would not depend on moral virtue, nor could there be a failure of the will, and there would be no problem of freedom of the will.

In its origins, the Enlightenment Project was intended to provide a secular rationale for liberal culture. By *liberal culture* is meant the concatenation of the technological project (conquest of nature), market economies, limited government, rule of law, individual rights, and toleration. There were two different endorsements. The first view, which is the origin of methodological individualism, assumed the truths of physicalism, empiricism, associationism, and intellectual hedonism. Because human nature partakes of the natural harmony of the universe, enlightened self-interest implies that human beings can manage their own affairs without government interference. As Randall put it:

> [S]ensationalism, associationism, hedonism, and intellectualism were ostensibly the outcome of a mechanical analysis of human nature. Actually, they were dictated by the demands of the middle class for social change. They became the philosophic justification of nineteenth-century British Liberalism, its method of criticizing traditional institutions, by their consequences in individual pleasures

and pains. They provided a rational basis for a society of laissez-faire and free competition, the trust in the reason of the common man."[11]

There is a second version of how the Enlightenment Project endorsed liberal culture. *Philosophes* such as Voltaire, Diderot, d'Alembert, and the physiocrats (Gournay, Quesnay, Turgot, and Dupont de Nemours) took their cue from Bacon. This latter group advocated not only the idea of the conquest of nature but also the idea of a social technology to solve all social and political problems. They equated this program with a powerful central government unencumbered by the Church, the courts, or legislative bodies. That is, they eschewed limited government. This second version is also avowedly liberal, but it would despite itself evolve into totalitarianism.

The clearest example of this is to be found in Helvétius' *De l'Esprit* (1758). Starting with Locke's epistemological claim that all knowledge originates in experience and that the human mind at birth is a tabula rasa, Helvétius goes on to embrace an extreme form of environmental determinism. This should remind us of Rawls' veil of ignorance. All differences in beliefs, attitudes, values, and so forth are solely the result of historical and environmental accident.[12] From this, it was concluded that all human beings were fundamentally identical and therefore equal. All forms of social hierarchy, privilege, and differences in power and influence were deemed the result of historical accident and denounced as unjust. In their place was substituted the notion that all individuals, when properly educated, were equally competent judges. Participatory democracy is therefore the only form of government compatible with the fundamental equality of human nature.

11. Randall, *The Career of Philosophy*, p. 924.

12. "Even the willingness to make an effort, to try, and so to be deserving in the ordinary sense is itself dependent upon happy family and social circumstances." John Rawls, *A Theory of Justice* (Cambridge: Harvard University Press, 1971), p. 74.

What Helvétius did not see was that his reading of Locke was also compatible with totalitarianism. First, if there were basic truths about human nature that dictated specific social arrangements then why should these practices not be forthwith instituted by a dictatorial and enlightened elite? Further, the people were to be trusted only if they were properly educated and had undergone a deprogramming therapy that cleansed them of the misperceptions from which they suffered as the result of previous oppressive governments. Allowing the people to debate public policy issues in their current state of mind ran the risk of their intellectual exploitation by scoundrels. It might be necessary to have a temporary dictatorship until the therapeutic process was completed, and even then political debate could be dispensed with in favor of scientific discussion among the informed experts followed by public reeducation.

Environmental determinism had also to be qualified by and made compatible with the assumption that a secularized natural law would continue to discover that all human beings shared the same basic goals. When these goals had been presumed to originate with God, as was the case in Locke and traditional natural law, it was not necessary to explain (1) why there were goals in the first place, (2) why these goals were common and universal to all human beings, and (3) why these goals could harmoniously coexist both within the same individual and among an entire community. Moreover, within traditional theologically based versions of natural law some consideration had been given to the inner conflicts we all experience and to potential social conflicts. Perfect justice was to be achieved in the next life, so that all we could hope for in this world was a harmony of private interests. When natural law is shorn of its theological framework, it becomes problematic why human beings should be believed to have natural goals at all, especially given a commitment to strong environmental determinism. It also becomes problematic to assume that if there were goals, they would be common to all human beings, especially in the presence of differing histories. Finally, and most important, how can there be scientific public policy and social reconstruction unless there is some natural harmony or guarantee of a lack of ultimate conflict?

Once the belief in God is surrendered, the adherence to a secularized natural law doctrine requires some substitute to guarantee the convergence toward a common interest. The logic of the argument will inevitably drive theorists to the conclusion that there must be a common or group interest that subsumes all of the individual interests so that ultimate fulfillment on the part of the individual can be achieved only within some absolute social and political framework. Modern totalitarianism is thus born. In that pivotal work, *What Is the Third Estate?*, the Abbe Sieyes had asserted that the nation "is prior to everything. It is the source of everything. . . . its will is always the supreme law."

Totalitarian democracy substitutes the idea of a collective good for the traditional idea of a harmony of interests. At the same time, it seemingly solves one of the serious problems of the new secularized natural law. Instead of having to establish that each individual has a built-in goal (as opposed to a historically acquired one) and instead of having to prove that each individual's natural goal is compatible with those of every other individual, the new totalitarian has merely to establish what the common goal is. Establishing this common goal was never done in any objective or scientific way, despite the scientific pretensions of the age. Instead, each and every revolutionary individual or faction was free to propose whatever was wanted.

The second version of the Enlightenment Project leads to a transformation of the Lockean conception of rights. In its Enlightenment Project form, the ends are not rights; rather, rights are means to the achievement of the ends. As such, rights are only prima facie, may be overridden, and may be possessed by any entity, not only individual human beings. Such rights can be welfare rights, that is, they may be such that others have a positive obligation to provide such goods, benefits or means. What distinguishes one social philosopher from another is (1) whether rights are understood to be absolute or prima facie, (2) the content of the rights, and (3) the lexical ordering of those rights.

All of the difficulties we have enumerated in the Enlightenment Project had been foreseen. Perhaps the most insightful critic of this kind of egalitarianism was David Hume. In one prescient paragraph in the *Enquiry Concerning the Principles of Morals*,[13] Hume stated the entire case against it. First, there was no agreement on what things should be equalized; that is, there was no consensus on which universal facts about human nature entailed normative social arrangements. Second, given that lack of agreement, demands for equality would remain nothing more than rhetorical masks for private political agendas. Third, even if it were possible to redistribute everything so that we all started out equal, differences in ability and circumstances (e.g., luck) would soon lead to inequalities. Fourth, and finally, to overcome the inegalitarian recidivism, it would be necessary to maintain the most all-encompassing social tyranny.

Notice that Hume is not objecting to equality before the law or equality of opportunity, forms of equality he supported. He supported them because they were part and parcel of a market economy in a commercial republic, that is, what we have called liberal culture. What he objected to was the allegedly scientific open-ended egalitarianism of the Enlightenment Project. Something new was also introduced in Hume's argument. The point of encouraging equality of opportunity is to maximize growth and the creation of greater opportunities, economic and otherwise, for everyone. The secular concern for growth has replaced the Reformation notion of doing God's work.

13. David Hume, *Enquiry Concerning the Principles of Morals* (Oxford: Clarendon Press, 1972), p. 194.

Nor was Hume alone in making such objections. Diderot dissented from Helvétius on the grounds that there were innate differences of ability as well as environmental influences. Probably neither the advocates of the Enlightenment Project nor their critics envisioned a genetic engineering that could presumably equalize genetic makeup.

Both Montesquieu and Edmund Burke shared one of Hume's concerns, the threat of tyranny. Both had maintained that some forms of social and economic hierarchy were a defense against tyranny, understood as the existence of a social order in which there were no intermediate institutions between isolated individuals and an all-powerful government needed to preserve the equality of the isolated individuals. This concern for a potential conflict between liberty and equality would resurface in the next century.

Rousseau represented an important and often overlooked and misunderstood countercurrent to the Enlightenment Project. Against the denial of the existence of a moral self, Rousseau reasserted it. Essentially he revived the Christian conception of the dignity of the individual soul but in a secular way. The kind of equality that counted, for him, was moral equality. He did recognize that this kind of equality could be threatened by economic inequality (*Discourse on the Origins of Inequality* in 1754) and in the *Social Contract* of 1762, where he urged that no one be "so rich as to be able to buy another, and none so poor as to have to sell himself."[14] However, he did not press for equality of political representation nor did he advocate the abolition of private property. Rather, he urged that there be something like an equal participation in the public good (general will).

Rousseau's views were developed by Kant into the notion of

14. Jean-Jacques Rousseau, "Social Contract," in *Political Writings of J. J. Rousseau*, edited by C. E. Vaughan (Cambridge, 1915), 2 vols.

autonomy and later by Hegel in the much more sophisticated reconciliation of civil society with the notion of a state. These views are reflected both in the current advocacy of self-respect and in the advocacy of self-esteem, about which we shall have more to say later. Even Bentham's utilitarian notion that each individual is to count as one and no more than one is another secular expression of this notion meant to cohabit the same space with the notion that individuals are only rational maximizers.

The French Revolution reflected all of the competing conceptions of equality we have identified. *The Declaration of Rights* of 1789 rejected privileges and opportunities based on birth and advocated equality of opportunity (access to public office should depend only on "virtues and talents"). It abolished feudalism, provided for equality of rights, equality before the law, equality of opportunity (abolished the inheritance of rank and public office), equality of punishment, equality of taxation. The abolition of slavery was proclaimed in 1794. All of this reflected the relative egalitarianism associated with a commercial republic, and this in turn reflected a secularized version of the Protestant Reformation within a market economy.

What was the perceived relationship between political equality and economic equality? There was no call for universal suffrage (not to be confused with equality before the law). The assumption was that political rights depended on achieving a certain minimal economic standing (property qualification).

"Grachus" Babeuf, on the other hand, whose first name is meant to remind us of the revolt led by the Grachhi brothers in ancient Rome, advocated an absolute equality. When informed that some people were more talented than others, he suggested that their right hands be cut off to equalize performance! He was the mastermind behind the Conspiracy of the Equals, designed to bring about total equality of outcome. He was executed in 1797.

NINETEENTH CENTURY

Nineteenth-century socialist thought represents a challenge to eighteenth-century thought on equality. The dominant eighteenth-century view was that political equality should reflect economic status. Specifically, those who were economically self-sufficient or capable of competing for economic benefits should be given political equality (equality of opportunity to compete, equality before the law, suffrage). Those who had to work for others in a fashion reminiscent of feudalism were deemed not self-sufficient. Nineteenth-century socialist thought, by and large, maintained that workers who appeared lacking in self-sufficiency were denied the opportunity to become self-sufficient. Economic inequality was held to be the fundamental inequality in that it was instrumental to all other forms of inequality (power, prestige, self-regard, self-sufficiency, etc.).

The so-called utopian socialists, including J. S. Mill, advocated ending the inequality of a society divided between employers and employees by making everyone a potential entrepreneur. To achieve this end, it would be necessary to provide the conditions for a minimally good life understood as the conditions necessary to render one self-sufficient—such as free public education. There is no notion here of the equality of outcome. It is thus a form of relative egalitarianism, only now it was recognized that in an industrial and commercial market economy, some form of economic redistribution might be necessary.

Marxists, on the other hand, sought to collapse the distinction between employer and employee by doing away with private property and entrepreneurship altogether. A collective good was to be realized in a planned and centrally organized economy. However, for Marx, true equality meant the advent of a classless society, not equality of income or function. "The real content of the proletarian demand for equality is the *abolition of classes*. Any demand for equality which goes beyond that, of necessity passes into absurdity."[15] There is no sentimental notion of equality in Marx, rather, a form of absolute egalitarianism. The workers would clearly not be equal to the planners, but it was assumed that this appearance of inequality would not be onerous or invidious in light of the collective good. Somehow or other differences of function would not translate into differences of status in light of the collective good.

The increasing call for an absolute equality, now understood as the call for the recognition of a collective good that subsumed the individual good, raised the same alarm that it had in the eighteenth century. Critics such as Tocqueville, Mill, and Burckhardt warned of a conflict between equality and liberty. The belief in and advocacy of a collective good in which individual good is subsumed do not see the necessity for preserving liberty. Rather they insist on controlling any institution and practice that contributes to individual fulfillment within the collective good. Defenders of liberty justify removing or relaxing external constraints because they presume that there is some kind of basic internal psychological need for something like personal autonomy. The defenders of liberty are reasserting in secular fashion the Christian doctrine of the dignity of the individual soul. This is what is behind J. S. Mill's defense of individuality.

The argument in favor of liberty and against absolute equality is sometimes presented as an efficiency argument. That is, the advocacy of economic equality in any absolute sense would lead to a severe net loss in economic benefits for all. Let us exhibit this loss.

In the following cases the value of the dollar and the inflation rate remain the same, and the number represents the annual income in U.S. dollars.

15. Karl Marx, *Anti-Dühring*, quoted from Abernethy, *The Idea of Equality*, pp. 199–200.

Society A	Society B₁	Society C	Society B₂
10% earn >$1,000,000	10% earn $100,000	10% earn $5,000,000	100% earn $250
70% earn $50,000	70% earn $49,000	70% earn $1,000,000	
20% earn $20,000	20% earn $22,000	20% earn $100,000	

The efficiency argument goes something like this. Society A represents where we are now. Society B_1 represents where we would be if current proposals for increasing the welfare state and redistributing income were put into effect. Society B_2 represents where we would be if absolute equality were imposed and maintained. Society C represents where we would be if we did away completely with income transfer schemes. Note that in Society C, the bottom 20 percent are much better off than they were in Society A in an absolute sense (remember the value or purchasing power of the dollar remains the same) but the gap between them and the middle 70 percent has grown wider. It might be pointed out that the numbers here are exaggerated. Even so, the point remains the same.

Defenders of absolute equality relative to a collective good must inevitably make the claim that even if there were a net loss of economic benefits, the noneconomic social benefits (e.g., the lack of envy) would far outweigh that loss. It has also been suggested that if the wealthy voluntarily chose to redistribute their wealth to the less wealthy or to the poor, there would be no loss of wealth and a lot less misery as well as more happiness. However, this suggestion fails to take into account that such a voluntary redistribution would affect future productivity. For example, a poor person is likely to spend the boon on immediate gratification whereas the wealthy person might reinvest that surplus in creating new industries and jobs. In fact three quarters of the wealth of the wealthiest individuals is invested in such ventures.

The argument in favor of liberty and against absolute equality is otherwise presented as an argument in favor of freedom or autonomy (understood here as self-rule). Even if there were no net economic loss, there would be an end to freedom of speech and eventually freedom of thought. We would see the triumph of mediocrity or a narrow public opinion imposing the same capricious and arbitrary standards on everything and everyone. These things are considered good because they are instrumental to self-expression and personal autonomy. For theorists like Mill, freedom trumps efficiency, and that is why he sometimes sounds like an absolute egalitarian. On the other hand, freedom also trumps equality, and in this respect we have returned to relative egalitarianism. Autonomy is an intrinsic end for relative egalitarians. Autonomy and liberty are not intrinsic ends for absolute egalitarians.

PRESENT

It is fair to say that the present situation of those who live in a liberal culture may be described as follows. We ignore for the sake of argument those who are unalterably opposed to liberal culture. Moreover, all those who are a party to this debate advocate relative equality, not absolute equality. For those of us who live in a liberal culture, we seem committed to the technological project, to the recognition of a free market economy as the best means for achieving it, to some notion of limited government as the best way to service the market economy, to the idea that government stays limited if there is the rule of law and some conception of rights. Where disagreements arise, they have arisen because of conflicting views of the human predicament. These conflicting views of the human predicament are reflected not only in different ideas about the status of rights and the meaning of the rule of law but also in conflicting views about equality. As we have already said, current disagreements about equality as a normative concept center on (1) factual claims about the specific sense or senses in which human beings are identical, (2) what constitutes relevant special treatment, that is, which specific senses carry normative weight, and (3) factual claims about which public policies are consistent and coherent with and effective in ensuring the relevant special treatment.

Let us begin with fundamental disagreements about the human predicament. I am going to present this as a disagreement between two poles with the recognition that there are intermediate positions. However, the intermediate positions are intelligible only because they operate between the two poles.

Advocates of the first pole (conception of equality that originated in Christianity and is represented in a modern secular context by Rousseau, Kant, Hegel, and Mill among others) maintain that there is some sense in which human beings are internally free and capable of being autonomous. This is the fundamental truth about human beings. As potentially free and autonomous beings, we have no specific goal to achieve or specific object that we need to possess. What is most important is the achievement of self-respect. Self-respect is not something that can be given from the outside. It is, instead, the recognition that we are internally capable of ruling ourselves and running our own lives. Personal autonomy is the ultimate good, and it is an individual possession. There is no such thing as a collective good. One of the important features about self-respect is that those who possess it want recognition from others who also possess it. It is this need for recognition (Hegel's argument) that obligates us to help others achieve personal autonomy and the self-respect that comes with it. Autonomy is not part of a zero-sum game, so that anyone's having it is not going to detract from others' having it. If anything, it thrives best in an infinitely expanding social universe.

Wealth is important not as an end in itself nor as a means to consumerism but because it serves as the means for personal accomplishment. Wealth maximization and efficiency considerations are important because in the end we need to know if such policies are maximizing opportunities for more and more people to become autonomous. Public policies that redistribute wealth are permissible to the extent that they ultimately promote autonomy. For example, equality before the law may require public legal aid schemes (e.g., Justice Black in *Griffin v. Illinois* in 1956) to ensure that everyone is properly represented in legal proceedings and not only those who can afford it. Equality of opportunity might require free public education to ensure that everyone is as well prepared to compete as is feasible. Notice that we said "might." All of these policies must be justified on the grounds that they promote autonomy and that they are efficient (vouchers might be more effective than government-run schools, mandatory legal insurance might be better than legal aid for most people, etc.) as well as not diminishing resources for other spheres in which human autonomy is important. It is always relevant to ask of any public policy if it works, if it is the only or best way to achieve our end, and whether it conflicts with other legitimate ends. Redistribution is not a priori objectionable, but the redistribution must be judged on whether it promotes autonomy as well as efficiency.

To sum up this first pole, autonomy (1) does not exist in degrees, (2) is not a zero-sum social game, (3) requires a minimum of social support that focuses on internal character, and (4) avoids interminable disputes about which lifestyles are better or more fulfilling.

One intermediate position worth identifying is the following. Human beings have neither a telos nor any ontologically meaningful sense of internal freedom. Human beings are individual bundles of needs and desires determined purely by human physiology (there is neither a unique psychological nor a spiritual domain). There is no objective reason or argument for why these needs ought to be equally satisfied. If we engage in policies of redistribution, the only reason is to maximize satisfactions through the creation of an expanding economic pie. The only consideration is efficiency.

Advocates of a second pole reflect the Enlightenment Project. They deny the existence of freedom in the sense of autonomy. They agree that human beings are individual bundles of needs and desires determined by human physiology. However, they also maintain that there is a special psychological need, namely, the need for fulfillment or self-esteem. We shall talk about self-esteem, but a few words on the fulfillment version are in order. Fulfillment sounds vaguely teleological and would have to be both identified and justified. Advocates of fulfillment also put more stress on the redistribution of wealth and tend not to want to get too involved in directing how people fulfill themselves.

Self-esteem is the much more interesting case. To have self-esteem is to have a positive self-image, and this self-image is a product of external environmental circumstances. If others look upon us as failures, as sociopaths, losers, or inferior, then our self-image suffers, we experience a deprivation of self-esteem, and a basic psychological need is not being met. Self-esteem is, therefore, by its very nature a relative concept.

Advocates of the second pole usually direct all of their criticism against the intermediate position and its emphasis on efficiency. Efficiency is equated with mere wealth maximization and the ignoring of the importance of self-esteem. One interesting example of this is Michael Young's claim, in *Rise of the Meritocracy*, that in a purely maximization and efficiency-driven system there will always be more losers than winners. In fact, the more honest, effective, and efficient the purely meritocratic system is, the more individuals will know they have no one to blame but themselves. The same sort of consequences are said to be implied by *The Bell Curve*. The end result will be enormous hostility.

Consequently, advocates of the second pole insist on the need for public policies that promote self-esteem. Such public policies involve at least two dimensions. First, there is the never-disappearing wealth gap that needs to be minimized; second, equal recognition must be given to all forms of human endeavor and not just to technology, the life of the mind, and so-called high-brow culture. Moreover, there is no final and definitive list of what has to be done to reach and preserve equality of self-esteem. This will always vary with changing circumstances. Finally, there is the recognition that to achieve or maintain equality it will be necessary to treat people unequally. As R. N. Tawney pointed out, the "more anxiously a society endeavours to secure equality of consideration for all its members, the greater will be the differentiation of treatment which . . . it accords to the special needs of different groups and individuals among them."[16] This will create a new set of privileges or inequalities, but these are said to be defensible given some ideal such as self-esteem. So, for example, affirmative action is alleged to be a justifiable form of reverse discrimination designed to secure equal rights for a group.

To sum up the second pole, advocates of the maximum fulfillment of potential or of self-esteem are (1) logically driven to equality of outcome, however outcome is defined, (2) are committed to maximum support, (3) must recognize that they are involved in a zero-sum game given the presence of finite resources, and (4) might be forced to define the maximization of human talent in terms of some conception of the social good (collectivist resolution).

Critics of the second pole generally repeat one or more of the criticisms made long ago by Hume: there is no consensus on what these subtle psychological needs are (e.g., Amartya Sen[17]); or they are the mere expression of private political agendas in a democratic context (e.g., envy syndrome or some other select list), that is, equality is a reflection of a larger social philosophy; whenever the equalization policies are put into effect, human beings will find some way to make the system unequal again (a point recognized by the advocates of the second pole, which is exactly why they claim that their job is never done); or, finally, we shall end up with a new

16. R. N. Tawney, *Equality* (New York: Capricorn Books, 1952), p. 39.
17. Amartya Sen, *Inequality Reexamined* (Cambridge: Harvard University Press, 1980).

class of tyrants who are the ones claiming to make all the adjustments on some social-scientific basis.

A good deal of contemporary discussion focuses on the people at the bottom, or what is called the *underclass,* the *less well off,* or the *disadvantaged.* The choice of descriptive term itself often reflects a preset analysis of these people. Part of the explanation for this focus is the religious heritage of the dignity of the human individual, even in a secular age. Some employ this focus because they believe that the existence of the poor discredits liberal culture or discredits the current policies toward the poor or those invested with the authority (as well as power and prestige) to deal with those issues. Some focus on the poor because their existence reflects wasted talent that impoverishes us all in a market economy. Some maintain this focus because it reflects the failure to promote autonomy in a segment of the community. It is this focus that reveals the conflicting estimates of appropriate public policy that flow from conflicting diagnoses of the problem. The issues of equality and poverty then are closely linked.

We conclude by calling attention to an important criticism of the second pole that did not appear in Hume. A contemporary advocate of the first pole, Michael Oakeshott in his essay *The Masses in Representative Democracy,* makes it. Although he does not specifically mention self-esteem, Oakeshott would identify the claims made on its behalf as examples of the social pathology of what he calls the *anti-individual.* Within liberal culture going back as far as the Renaissance and the Reformation, many people have not made the transition to individuality. There is a complicated history behind this, but what is important is to recognize that the most serious problem within modern liberal societies is the presence of the anti-individual. Being an anti-individual is a state of mind. It is not directly correlated with income, intelligence, or how articulate you are. Some anti-individuals are highly intelligent. Either unaware of or lacking faith in their ability to exercise self-discipline, the anti-individual seeks escape into the collective identity of communities insulated from the challenge of opportunity. These are people focused on avoiding failure rather than on achieving success. Phenomenologically speaking, the anti-individual can identify herself or himself by feelings of envy, resentment, self-distrust, victimization, and self-pity—in short, an inferiority complex.

What really inhibits these people is not a lack of opportunity, not a lack of political rights, and not a lack of resources but a character defect, a moral inadequacy. Having little or no sense of individuality they are incapable of loving what is best in themselves. What they substitute for love of self, others, and family is loyalty to a mythical community. Instead of an umpire they want a leader, and they conceive of such leaders as protectors who relieve them of all responsibility. This is what makes their sense of community pathological. What they end up with are leaders who are their mirror image: leaders who are themselves anti-individuals and who seek to control others because they cannot control themselves, who seek the emasculation of autonomous individuals, who prize equality and not competition. In place of a market economy and limited government, we get economic and political tyranny.

CHAPTER TWO

Liberty and Equality— A Question of Balance?

Jan Narveson

THE QUESTION

Liberty and equality have been discussed over and over, by countless writers, and those discussions have been generally inconclusive. That is not too surprising, really. For one thing, the discussants are rarely very clear about what exactly their subject is, and so confusion is virtually inevitable. For another, the discussion tends to proceed by simply proclaiming principles rather than by trying to find a fundamental basis for them; consequently, the incompatible conclusions reached by different discussants are immune to rational rebuttal or qualification, again making disagreement unsurprising. Finally, discussants typically have special interests, axes to grind, which also impedes sober analysis and responsible, objective reasoning. Perhaps it is too much to hope that the treatment undertaken here will succeed where others have failed, but it is certainly worth a try.

Actually, the verdict that failure is general is, in a way, too pessimistic. The conclusions of this chapter are certainly not new, though it is hoped that they will emerge more clearly from this treatment. Their lack of novelty is, for that matter, something of a recommendation, but still we must never accept a view only because it is of long standing. When a general, fundamental principle of society is widely acknowledged in practice by ordinary people over a very long period, I take that to suggest that it probably has something going for it; but it is not, itself, proof. Rather, that fact suggests that there are real underlying reasons for it, and its durability is due to those reasons, not the other way around.

Our subject is the proper "balance" between liberty and equality, a formulation of the question that suggests, without strictly entailing, that both have their claims and that what is needed is a fine-tuned proportion of the one and the other. But that is misleading, as we shall see. Indeed, it is so misleading that insofar as there is anything clear in it, I will, in fact, be denying it, arguing instead that in its proper domain, we do have a general right to liberty and consequently do not have a fundamental right to equality, of any interesting kind. A popular contemporary philosopher has proclaimed that if there really were a conflict between equality and liberty, equality would have to win.[1] What I suggest is that just the opposite is closer to the truth, once one looks carefully at these ideas.

This conclusion implies, of course, that the two are rivals, a view that has been frequently and fervently denied by various recent writers, including the author of the foregoing dictum.[2] We cer-

---

1. Ronald Dworkin, "The Place of Liberty," in *Sovereign Virtue* (Cambridge: Harvard University Press, 2000), pp. 120–183.

2. Other authors who claim to reconcile the two are Kai Nielsen, *Equality and Liberty: A Defense of Radical Egalitarianism* (Totowa, N.J.: Rowman and Allanheld, 1985); and Richard Norman, *Free and Equal* (Oxford: Oxford University Press, 1987). For a set of essays expressing many shades of opinion on the subject, see *Equality and Plurality*, ed. by Larry May, Christine Sistare, and Jonathan Schonsheck (Lawrence: University Press of Kansas, 1997). (One of the essays is mine: "Liberty, Equality, and Distributive Justice," pp. 15–37.)

tainly need to clear that up. There are different issues to be distinguished here, and so the question whether the two are rivals or not cannot be answered, straight off, with a flat "Yes" or "No." However, when the dust is settled, what we will see is that the answer, in the main and most perspicuous sense of the question, is: yes, they are incompatible—and that between them, we should prefer liberty to equality.

DEFINITIONS AND CLARIFICATIONS

Let us start, then, by making some of the needed distinctions and clarifications. To begin with, our question has to do with the constitution or basic organization of society, the underlying principles that make it work. Thus, the liberty we are discussing is that between human and human, rather than between human and mosquito, or human and volcano. Doubtless there are many things we would like to be free from: cancer, debt, fear of toads, and, for that matter, mosquitoes and volcanoes. But in moral and political contexts, the subject of liberty concerns interference by some people with some other people's intended actions and plans of action. People are at liberty in this regard when other people do not so interfere, whatever the germs or the faultlines may have to do with it; they are not at liberty, of the kind we are talking about here, insofar as other people interfere.

We can and should be a bit more precise here. We can interfere with liberty in two ways. One is by making it simply impossible for the other person to do what he or she wanted, as when we tie someone to a tree. The other is by making it costlier to the other. We do that when we threaten: "Hand it over, or I'll shoot!" Your not handing it over then becomes much more costly to you than it was before. That is coercion, which interferes with liberty just as outright use of force does. Indeed, we may generally define liberty, as a recent author has done, as the absence of imposed costs.[3]

Should we hold that liberty is, somehow, desirable? And for whom? The questions are, again, misleading. Liberty is the absence of hindrances from doing what the hindered person thinks is desirable on its own, or some other account. Liberty is not like that: it is not like chocolate or Chopin. If we did not care about anything, then the liberty to do it would not be of any value whatever. The liberty to do what we might care about, though we do not at this very moment want to, is indeed valuable, but it is valuable because it may enable us to realize some other value or because we may perhaps change our minds about the one in question. This being so, we cannot sensibly discuss the value of liberty, simply as such: it is by definition valuable if anything that we might be able to accomplish by action is, but not in the same way as those things themselves. It is valuable because it is indispensable to those pursuits, which in turn are what make life worth living. Liberty is not just another good, then, like a new suit. In the sense in which liberty is the absence of disabling obstacles to action, it is a precondition of anyone's doing anything whatever, and so of anyone's doing any good thing. In the sense in which it is the absence of other imposed costs, liberty is a precondition for doing precisely what you wanted, rather than doing what you wanted plus various other things (such as paying sales tax) that you do not want. So liberty in general is a precondition for all efficient action.

Another way in which the question is misleading is that in a sense we are not mainly discussing whether liberty is desirable, but instead whether we should think that people have a right to it, and that is not the same thing. Now, it is plausible to suppose that whether we have rights to this or that is a question that can be

---

3. Jan Lester, *Escape from Leviathan* (New York: St. Martin's Press, 2000). See especially pp. 58–61.

pursued only by inquiring whether it would, in turn, be valuable, desirable, worthwhile, to attribute rights of that kind to people and to proclaim and defend those rights on all our behalfs. Even so, the question whether it is valuable to award a right of this or that kind to someone is quite different from that of the value of the things someone might have if he or she does have that right. Chocolate, the symphonies of Mahler, and a walk in the woods on a fine day are all good things, and for that very reason, we want to be free to have an occasional chocolate, attend performances of Mahler, and take a walk in the woods if we are so inclined. But it is not clear what it would even mean to say that the liberty to take a walk in the woods, as distinct from the walk itself, is intrinsically good.

It is, however, quite clear what it means to say, or to deny, that we have a right to do those things; or at any rate, if there are any respects in which it is not clear, we can make it clear enough by providing context. For example, I do not have a right to walk in *your* woods without your permission, to attend the symphony performance without buying a ticket, or to help myself to the chocolate on the counter at your shop. Yet for all that, a government that forbade, across the board, eating chocolate, listening to Mahler, or walking in the woods would be acting wrongly and violating the rights of its citizens, whereas the organizers of the symphony concert and the producers of the chocolate act rightly and violate no rights when they charge for their services.

Put in those terms, the answer to whether there is a right to liberty is easy: yes. And the question of who has this general right is also easily answered: we all do. There are, indeed, important questions concerning the reach of everyone: are infants in arms also to be thought to have a right to liberty or something of the sort? We will not be able to devote attention to that very interesting subject; getting straight about what grownups do and do not owe other grownups is the first order of business and the only one we will pursue in this short inquiry.

LIBERTY LIMITED BY LIBERTY

Much more important and more difficult is the question of the scope of liberty. The liberty to do anything whatever that we might conceivably want to do is valuable to the would-be doer, no doubt, be he or she a philanthropist, a ditch-digger, or an assassin. But it is inherently impossible for everyone to have the right to do all those things: many things that someone might want to do will have the effect of denying some liberty to someone else, and unless a fairly clear formula can be found for picking out who must give way in such cases, the idea of general liberty will be useless.

But, fortunately, there is a tolerably clear formula, implicit perhaps in what has already been said: the principle of liberty says that those whose actions do not adversely affect others are entitled, have a right, to noninterference insofar as that is so, whereas those actions that do interfere with innocent others are, again prima facie, in the wrong, and not to be permitted. Only via such a distinction is the idea of a universal right to general liberty possible.

RIGHTS

Having mentioned rights, we move now to defining that notion. First, and centrally, a right is a status entailing that certain other persons lie under a duty toward the rightholder, in regard to the matters over which he or she has that right. This duty is, at a minimum, the duty to refrain from what would impose costs or obstacles to the doing of what he or she has a right to: those on whom that duty follows are not to worsen the situation of the rightholder in those respects. Rights that entail only duties to refrain are called "negative rights." Another sort of rights, called "positive rights," imposes the duty not only to refrain, but also to do something by way of enabling the rightholder to do what he or she is being said to have the right to do. More will be said about that later.

It is often said that rights entail responsibilities, but that is an indirect point. So far as a right is a right, and no more, it does not entail responsibilities, but rather, freedom on the part of the right-holder and responsibilities and duties on the part of other people. It is their rights that, in turn, impose duties and responsibilities on the rightholder himself or herself.

On which others do these duties fall? That must be specified and explained by the claimant. Is it everybody? Or just Jim Doakes? Or the people of South Dakota? It could be any of those, or indefinitely many other possible sets of persons. The person making the claim that someone has a right will have to explain this. However, when we are discussing the *basic* rights of people in general, then the duties they impose are imposed on everybody. When rights are general, that is, held by all, then my rights impose duties on you and your rights impose duties on me.

Second, rights are advantageous to the rightholder; he or she must expect to be better off with it than without it and better off if others respect it than if they do not. You cannot have the right to be tortured, just like that, but you could have the right to have your sadomasochistic partner whip you if, for some odd reason, that is what you want. But then you are (oddly) viewing this as a benefit, rather than a detriment. (Of course, it is possible to misuse one's liberty, ending up a drunk, for example. But that possibility is not sufficient reason for depriving people of liberty in the first place.)

Third, rights are enforceable. So, although rights are advantageous to the people who have them, they are, on the face of it, a disadvantage to the people who are required to respect them. We must emphasize the word *required:* a right is something the others must respect so that if they do not, then force may be brought into play, if necessary, to see to it that they comply. So rights are different from mere recommendations, or statements of ideals. The mountain climber determined to get to the top is ready to strain every nerve, exert himself to the utmost, to get there; yet nobody may force him to do this. But he may not get there by trampling on others on the way up, or stealing their equipment—that would violate those people's rights. Rights are constraints on other people, and their rights, in turn, are constraints on us; they prevent us from doing certain things.

We may add that there has to be some reason, some basis for attributing the right in question to the individual in question: what is it about him or her that grounds or supports the claim that he or she has this duty? That subject must be explained by the theorist of rights, who needs to explain why this fact about the proposed right-holder is such as to impose a duty on those over, or against, whom he or she has this right. And, if he or she is to have a plausible theory, he or she had better explain why these other people, who are imposed on by it, should put up with this.

Now, interference with others is itself an action, and the worrying prospect arises, when we contemplate the idea of a perfectly general right to liberty, that it involves a contradiction. For a general right to liberty would seem to imply a right of everyone to the liberty to interfere with others, and indeed, any or all others; yet interference is precisely what a right to liberty forbids. Resolving this is obviously an important matter, and a very thorny one.

NEGATIVE AND POSITIVE RIGHTS

This right not to interfere is called a "negative right," so called because the duty of noninterference is a duty to refrain from doing something—a duty not to do something, rather than a duty to do something. We may also formulate the concept of a "positive right." That would be a right giving others the duty not only to refrain from interfering but also to assist Alice in doing what she is being said to have a right to do, at least if Alice is not able to do X herself.[4] Negative rights are rights entailing duties to refrain; positive rights are rights entailing duties to do, to take positive action to benefit the rightholder.

Now recall that rights are invoked with a view to enforcement. If you have a right to do something, then others must desist, or must assist, and we, society (or the legal system as the case may be) may, and perhaps should, compel the reluctant dutyholder to get with it. Rights then, curtail, and indeed that is their point: they are designed to curtail certain freedoms, namely, the freedom to do what someone else's right decrees may not be done. The principle of liberty is a self-limiting one: it limits liberty for the sake of liberty.

This being so, it is obviously of crucial importance whether the issue designated by this chapter's title concerns rights or something else. It is easy to say, heedlessly, that equal this or equal that would be a good thing—the nation should be ashamed if it has not provided it—and so forth. But that is a much different question from the question of rights, which is where we came in. It does not matter how good something is if bringing it about involves violating somebody's rights. This thought is one that advocates of ideals have a tendency not to think, so intent are they about their ideals. But they should.

LIBERTY AND EQUALITY

If it concerns rights, then the discussion is narrowed to the issue of whether we have rights to liberty or to equality. But this would not

4. The reader is recommended not to turn to the celebrated writings of Sir Isaiah Berlin on this distinction. I defy anyone to get a clear idea of the distinction Sir Isaiah urged between what he called positive and negative liberty, which should be a parallel distinction. See his oft-republished "Two Concepts of Liberty," in *Four Essays on Liberty* (London and New York: Oxford University Press, 1969)

even be interesting if what was in question was merely a negative right to it. For of course you are welcome to try to make yourself equal to your neighbor, or somebody in Australia, or whomever, as long as your neighbor does not have to go along with it. And if the right is merely negative, then, of course, he or she does not have to go along with it.

But that is obviously not what egalitarians have in mind. They proclaim a right to equality such that others must give them this equality. The egalitarian will divide whatever he or she thinks should be equal and see to it that nobody gets more or less. If, of course, what the egalitarian wants to distribute equally is money or various other things (such as opportunity, which we will discuss shortly), then this will involve cutting down to size those with more, in order to shore up the position of those with less, something not usually welcomed by those with more.

And so the sense of opposition becomes clear. Rights to equality that are in fact proposed are positive rights, which entail that some people may be compelled to become equal or more nearly equal with others in the respect in which equality is proclaimed. And whatever the sort of equality in question is (with one supposed exception, to be discussed next), it will conflict with a right to liberty, because liberty is doing what one pleases, and if people do not please to be made more equal in the respect in question, then asserting a right to equality is incompatible with asserting a right to the liberty in question. If you have a positive right to equality from K and J, then K and J do not have the right to refrain from giving it to you. In one and the same matter, as Thomas Hobbes observes, liberty and obligation are inconsistent: if you are at liberty to do something or not, as you please, then you are not obliged to do one or the other, and if you are obliged to do one or the other, then you are not at liberty to do whichever you like.

EQUAL LIBERTY?

Now for the aforementioned supposed exception to my finding of incompatibility: some have insisted that the political and moral outlook known as libertarianism is, after all, a form of egalitarianism, namely, one that specifies that what is to be equal is liberty. Is this an interesting truth about that view, or is it essentially a dodge—or a reduction of the issue to triviality?

Whether it is interesting, I shall now point out, depends on two things. First, it depends on whether a negative or a positive right to liberty is what is in question. A positive right to liberty would entail on all of us the duty to promote liberty, not merely the duty to respect it. The promotion of liberty goes far beyond merely allowing people to be at liberty. My duty if I believe that everyone has a general right to negative liberty is to refrain from interfering with others' doing as they please, living the way they wish. But if I believe that I have a duty to promote liberty, then I believe that I have the duty to do something, perhaps as much as I can, to bring it about that others not previously at liberty now are so. The difference that makes could, and probably would, be enormous. For in all likelihood, at any given time plenty of people would find themselves with their right to general liberty infringed or violated by somebody or other. And perhaps I could, with a great deal of trouble, help some of those people, by exerting myself to loosen the grip of their oppressors on them. But if we have only a negative right of liberty, then I will not be obligated to help anybody else, nor they me. People who oppress me are in the wrong, and I can complain and take action to undo their oppression, but I also have the right to sit back and be my oppressors' willing slaves, come to that; likewise to sit back while they oppress *you*. So, as I say, it does make a great difference which view one is proposing.

So much difference does it make that many discussions of the subject are vitiated when we invoke the distinction at the appropriate point. Those, for example, who insist that the distinction of negative and positive rights is illusory or otherwise mistaken do so on the ground that the enforcement of either sort of right can take positive action. That is true, but it does not establish the point, because if what we have is a pure negative right, then nobody has, so far as that goes, the duty to enforce it, or to rectify the actions of those who violate it. We do not show that there is no difference between a positive right and a negative right by adding to the negative right a positive right to its enforcement. All we do is muddy the waters.

Let us be perfectly explicit about it. Recall that a right is a status such that some set of other people lie under a duty toward the rightholder in regard to the matters to which the rightholder has that right. But a duty to do what? One sort of duty is a duty not to do various things, such as to assault the rightholder or put land mines in his or her path as he or she sets about doing what he or she has the right to do. A quite different sort is the duty to render some kind of assistance to the rightholder. The first kind—the negative duty—does not entail the second. I can refrain from helping you even as I also refrain from harming you—no problem.

Now, with this in mind, let us note that in regard to negative rights, the notion of equality is fairly uninteresting. To say that one thing is equal to another is to say that the two are variable in degree, somehow measurable, and such that the degree in each case is the same. But how are we to apply such a notion to a non-doing? Of course, we can say that the right of all to the nonviolence of others is equal in the sense that the amount of violence anyone is allowed to do is the same as the amount that anyone else is allowed to do, namely, none. But there is no question here of equalizing anything. Violence (against the innocent) is to be eliminated, not to bring it about that we all engage in the same amount of it, but because violence against innocents is wrong—wrong no matter how much of it anybody else does. My murder does not become justified by the fact that I am only murdering the same number of victims as the others; we are *all* in the wrong. Communism in the twentieth century, we are told, was responsible for almost one hundred million deaths. Well, each and every one of those deaths was wrongful. The Stalinist secret policeman murdering his hundredth victim was doing a wrong, even though the person he was murdering is getting the same treatment as the other ninety-nine.

EQUAL TREATMENT

When do we have a right to equal treatment? All of us always have the general right that others not kill, torture, maim, hobble, or otherwise damage us; nobody has this right any more than anyone else, and indeed it scarcely makes sense, as we have seen, to claim that this is a matter of degree. What could be a matter of degree is the amount of police protection you get, for example. And indeed it is a problem just how much police protection one or another person is entitled to, if we think they are entitled to any. If we give everyone equal protection in the sense that each gets fifteen minutes' worth of police attention per week, then are those for whom that is not nearly enough, because they will soon be dead in that case, really getting an equal right to liberty the same as those living in Lake Park, Minnesota, who would have no idea what to do with all that attention?

In any case, here again the waters are easily muddied by begging the question. Do we have a positive right to any protection at all? We have the right that others not murder us. If some people insist on trying to violate that right, it behooves their intended victims—us, perhaps—to protect themselves and probably to enlist others to help out. But it is not clear that there is any right to any particular amount of protection. It depends on the arrangement and the circumstances. Neither you nor I have a duty to join the nearest police force to protect people's rights. (Mind you, all of us pay taxes to maintain the police. Is it right that we be compelled to do so? That is certainly a question of great interest, but not one we can address here, unfortunately.)

For talk of equality to be significant in the present context, we need to be clear about four things. First, exactly what is it that is to be equally distributed? Second, among which set of persons is it to be so? Third, are we claiming a right to this sort of equality, or only that we think it would be a nice thing? And if it is a right, then, fourth, is it a negative right or a positive right? These questions make all the difference, which is why I said at the outset that one could not simply answer the topic's question with a simple "Yes" or "No."

If the claim to a right to equality is not being made, then there is no problem. We are all entitled to our views about what the "ideal society" would look like, but we are not entitled to do whatever we think necessary to bring it about. Indeed, we are entitled to do only those things that enlist the voluntary cooperation of others, not only the others in one's gang of terrorists, but all others.

But suppose the proponent is serious about this, and thinks that people generally have a right to equality of something, something real and nontrivial, not merely "equal concern and respect," as one modern writer has put it,[5] but, say, equal income, or equal time on the radio, or equal numbers of hours of medical care. Here we need to ask two questions: First, why that? And second, simply, why?

The question why here is a serious one. It is not answered adequately by jumping up and down, waving brightly colored banners, and shouting "Vive l'égalité!" Instead, the proponent must explain, in some quite convincing way, why we and everybody should be on that bandwagon. And if he cannot do that, then he is saying that

5. Dworkin, "The Place of Liberty."

a bunch of armed men get to come to our doors at 4:00 A.M. and march us down to the local prison if we do not surrender whatever it is that we have a supposedly unfairly unequal amount of, no questions asked or answered. But that is the sort of thing that needs justifying. Having the Grand Commissar of the Drug Laws stand up and proclaim that drugs are bad for you is not enough. It is grotesquely not enough to justify the incarceration of four hundred thousand people every year. Indeed, it is not enough to justify the incarceration of *anybody*. In like manner, the fact that I or you or somebody has a bit more of some desirable thing than someone else has is no justification for official bullies coming to extract it from us and hand it over to somebody else who happens to have less of it.

Well, when do we have a right to equal treatment, to equality? Never? Quite the contrary. There are often quite good reasons for insisting that somebody has the right to be treated equally, in some quite determinate way, with someone else.

First, if Smith has a justified claim to X, and Jones a justified claim to a like amount of X, then the two have an equal right to X. But how much X do they have a right to, and why? On occasion, there is a good answer. If you and I and Olson have all signed the same contract, with the same terms, then we may be each entitled to $X, the same for each. Positive rights founded on agreements to just the terms in question have satisfactory, indeed, impeccable, credentials. But clearly, you and I have not signed anything to the effect that we all owe a certain amount for Social Security, a certain amount for everybody's schooling, and so on. If you are going to assert a general positive right, a right of all, to the same amount of something, we would have to look elsewhere for its basis.

So where will we look? Can we look to some law, some act of government? Governments are composed of people, and people are fallible; they may be right, they may be wrong. For a bunch of people in some big impressive building to get together and decide to gouge us all to support some presumably worthy cause is tantamount to R. Hood & Co. deciding whom to rob so as to contribute wealth to the poor. The fact that he was able to round up enough bowmen to do the job hardly shows that it was right.

On the other hand, if we are (as we all are these days) under the thumb of government, then the laws will say who is supposed to get what, and then we can find that often they call for an equal amount of dollars, or something, for all of certain sorts of people. Insofar as we are subject to those rulings, we can often claim that someone was inequitably treated—given the law, he or she should have had as much as so-and-so and he or she did not get it.

But as I say, the prior question is what the government should be doing, and often the answer is nothing. It is at this most basic level that we want to pursue the subject, and so appeal to the existing law is of limited use here.

What about the rewards of labor and other virtuous activities? Do we not owe people equity in wages, for example? Not very much, as it will turn out on close inspection. The slogan "Equal Pay for Equal Work!" is still trotted out often enough in contexts of pay equity. But on closer inspection, this slogan comes to very little. To see this, first ask, how do you measure work? We do not measure work in hours: one worker's hour of work maybe worth many times another's. Nor is work measured in calories; the executive at his desk may be doing far more of value than an incredibly active lumberjack who requires six steaks a day to keep his strength up. Worse yet, exactly the same duration of exactly the same labor may be worth virtually nothing at some times and places and a great deal at others. A skilled mechanic in Calcutta makes perhaps a twentieth the salary of a similarly skilled mechanic in Santa Monica, California, and rightly so. Everything is wrong with the idea that people have a right to equal pay for equal work, as that slogan would be realized in any kind of law you could dream up. The slogan is not even a truism; it is, more precisely, a falsism. We negotiate with employers and employees, we strike the best deal we can, and we then owe what we have agreed to: employees owe their employers certain services, and the employers in turn owe them what was agreed on.

Consider us consumers. Do we have a right to equal prices from the various businesses that supply us with food or household wares? We do not. All we can say is that if someone can produce X for less money than someone else, that someone else had better do something about it or he or she will not long be in business. But is there a duty to price equally, a right on our part to such equal prices? Far from being a basic moral truth of some sort, it is an absurdity.

What is true, only, is this: from the point of view of the employer, an equal contribution to the profitability of the firm should, and likely will, earn its contributor an approximately equal level of pay. That entails nothing that can reasonably find its way into legislation, though it tells the worker a lot about what he or she should do to command a higher wage.

In short, you are entitled to what your employer has signed on the dotted line for your case, whatever it is, provided only that the print wasn't too small. Accordingly, you are well advised to make the best deal you can. No sort of claim on anyone else's money, advanced in absence of a plain agreement with that person, has a leg to stand on by comparison with the agreement itself, and that means that we have no interesting and fundamental principle of equality underlying pay rates, except the principle of keeping our agreements. It's the other way around, rather: market forces push the wages for recognizably similar kinds of labor toward recognizably similar levels, though almost always without ever actually reaching an equilibrium.

FAIRNESS, INCOME, AND WEALTH

There is a familiar attitude, written into many learned treatises of the day, to the effect that disparities of wealth are unfair. Is there anything to this? When are we being unfair to someone? And even when we are, is that necessarily unjust? For that matter, do we owe everyone the duty of fairness?

Fairness presupposes that we have a number of people who qualify for the distribution of a certain type of good and are therefore entitled to some share of it. But does being fair require that we should give everyone an equal share? Certainly not; indeed, it does not require that even among those who are entitled to some of it. Suppose a number of people work together on some project, voluntarily, and everyone contributes to it. Should everyone have an equal share of the resulting product? Not likely; some people will contribute more than others. When making a movie, everyone involved should not get the same amount: the stars who make movies successful by their very presence as well as their dramatic gifts, should (and do) make more than the technicians, gaffers, gofers, and others involved. The general formula for dividing the product is that each person receives his or her marginal product: all other things constant, how much difference does this person contribute to the total product? People who are not members of the team are not entitled to any of its product, and among those who are, the ones who contribute more deserve to get more, and usually do. They get it because if they do not, they are quite likely to go elsewhere where their contributions are better appreciated.

Those who preach the gospel of general equality seem positively determined to ignore the question of where the good things they want to distribute came from in the first place. They speak, remarkably often, as though wealth and services just grow on trees. But of course, they do not. Almost everything we have is made by someone; even things not made are made available to us by the efforts of other people, including, for that matter, the very things that do grow on trees, because somebody has to cultivate and harvest and ship the products. Those productive efforts are highly variable among people, but many people invest a great deal of effort in making what they do. To claim an equal share irrespective of contribution is to claim the right to exploit, and at the extreme to enslave, one's fellows.

This is not to deny that some fortunes have been made by theft, fraud, connivery, and the like. The point is not that all disparities of wealth are justified, but that many are. What justifies them is that the people with more have earned it by honest means, basically, by performing useful services for other people, services those other people have found it worthwhile to pay for at prices that led to high incomes for those who supplied those services. This is as it should be and has little to do with how one person's income compares with another.

EQUAL OPPORTUNITY

This brings up the subject of equal opportunity, a slogan with a wide following in this day and age. But again, a modest amount of reflection casts doubt on arguments of distributive justice along this line. The basic problem is, once again, that opportunities do not grow on trees but are created by particular people. Current political rhetoric suggests that some people are denying others certain opportunities—blacks and women are frequent examples— and that this is unfair. But opportunities exist only because of the efforts of the people who create those opportunities: inventors invent, entrepreneurs spot opportunities, investors fund them, and so on. Once Ms. A has gone to the trouble to create a situation in which someone else can usefully fill a job, there is no reason why A must give it to just anyone. Those who create the opportunity are the ones entitled to choose whom to give that opportunity to—whom to employ, for example. The entrepreneur does not owe anyone else a job. So the claim that there is a right to equal opportunity begs a question and confuses an issue. As so often, the case for equality turns on confusion; everyone has the same right to a given opportunity as anyone else only in the sense that none of us has any (positive) right to it at all—no one has a duty to extend opportunities equally to everyone or anyone. But that is hardly what those who embrace the slogan have in mind, though it is the only sense in which it is true. We do not, for example, have an obligation to prepare people equally for life, say, by educating them. We ought to do that for our children, yes, but for everybody?

For one thing, preparing people for opportunities is difficult, and the preparation is quite specific to the sort of opportunities envisaged. The goatherd on the slopes of Grecian mountainsides will, quite properly, teach his children very differently from what a professor at Stanford might teach her children; and likely, very soon, she in turn will teach each of her children quite differently, depending on their abilities, inclinations, and circumstances. We cannot really tell people very well how to raise their children, and we certainly cannot claim to know how to bring up every person. People are so different, in skills, physical and psychological capacities, interests, and life circumstances that it would be generally pointless even to try.

The point is worth taking a little further. The most vocal proponents of equal opportunity are generally educators and, as we may say, intelligentsia. That is not too surprising, really, because even though the intelligent are the very people who are in the best position to know how different people are, what different pieces of knowledge those different people might need or want, and how impossible it is even to compare one person's opportunities with another's, yet they are also the people who will benefit if huge amounts of money extracted from unwary taxpayers are devoted to this worthy-sounding cause. The training they have in mind is mostly of the sort that they themselves try to provide; never mind that different academics provide such different fare that a typical academic is almost totally ignorant of what almost all of his or her colleagues, especially those on the far reaches of campus, might be able to teach—we each know a dollar when we see one. But that is not a credible basis for proclaiming a right to the taxpayer's money. The cause for which it is to be spent is basically absurd; equal opportunity, to put it bluntly, is either indefinable or impossible, and usually both.

THE RIGHT TO TAKE ADVANTAGE

OF OPPORTUNITIES

The only reasonable meaning for the equal opportunity principle is that no one may intervene to prevent people from taking legitimate opportunities they are freely offered. Yet in general, it is government action billed as promotive of equal opportunity that undercuts precisely that. If in the interests of equal opportunity some government forbids Jones to take a voluntarily made offer from Smith, then that government has denied Jones an opportunity, and denied Smith the opportunity to extend someone else an opportunity. Governments often intervene in this way, particularly in offices such as immigration: foreigners will be denied the chance to work in a Canadian job, simply because they are foreigners, even when Canadian employers want to offer them those jobs. And these denials are indeed wrong. But they are wrong not because of a vague principle of a right to equal opportunity, but because of a specific principle that we have no business preventing people from peaceably seeking to better their lives.

The problem with equal opportunity as a slogan is the usual thing: it sounds good until you realize what it means. No one denies that opportunity is a good thing, and it is wonderful when opportunities are widely available, and perhaps, on occasion, even equally available in some meaningful sense: let's take the whole class to the zoo, say. But there is everything wrong with introducing compulsion into the equation, and when you scratch it, that is what the slogan really means. Equal opportunity, as it is brandished in political contexts, says, "Let's force A, who wants to offer an opportunity to B, to offer it to C, D, and E as well." Never mind whether these other persons are relevant, or interested, or whether A has any particular reason to extend the offer to them. And who pays the bill for making all those extra offers, vetting all those applications, and so on? Why, A, of course! This means that if he manages to survive in business, his customers, or, of course, taxpayers, must foot the bill. People who brandish slogans such as these are all ready to put hobbles on any number of people in order to realize their political ends, which, in the end, consist mainly of expanding their own political power. But they are realized at the expense of individual people trying to live their own lives, as best they can. Yet individual people doing the best they can is what the whole political system is *for.*

RANK AND STATUS: SOCIAL EQUALITY

Many of the immigrants who came to the United States and Canada were motivated, in considerable part, by a desire to get out from under the oppressive atmosphere of social classes. In Europe, there were aristocrats of many levels, and they looked down on the middle class people who in turn looked down on working class people and servants. If you were in any but the top class, you were likely to resent these attitudes. But along with the attitudes, subtly or otherwise, went many other things too. Aristocrats often had not only social status but also power. Those beneath them toed the line because of what the aristocrats could do to them if they did not.

I think it generally true to say that in North America we have little sense of class. The aesthetic leaders would agree, and deplore it: they think we lack discernment, taste, and discrimination between what is good and what is bad in the arts, especially. But in America, people need not pay any attention. And in any case, the aesthetic upper class does not correlate well with wealth or any of the other familiar measures of class. The upper classes in America are for the most part creatures of fad, the newspapers, the entertainment industry, and social custom that is not taken very seriously. What Americans especially think, I believe, is that nobody has the right to treat others as social inferiors, that those who actually try to treat other people thus are being silly or offensive. And they are right, of course. Very wealthy people in America often make a point of being just plain folks like the rest of us, only with more expensive cars, houses, and vacations.

The phenomenon of class, once it is detached from the sort of political system typified by the *ancien régime*, is an intriguing and rather puzzling thing. It is also something readily avoided by most of us. It tends to go with wealth, but it does not go very far. You are entitled to become extremely wealthy, but you are not entitled to think it gives you the right to order the rest of us around, because it does not. Many of us look up to some people for their accomplishments—baseball players, violinists, Nobel Prize winners—and we admire others for their looks, their wit, their sense of style, and any number of other things. It would be absurd to insist that in so doing we violate some kind of basic rights. Joshua Bell is a better violinist than you or I, almost no matter who you are; I could not beat Michael Schumacher around a racetrack no matter how hard I tried—he is simply a better driver than you or I. But in the United States (and Canada, where I live) we have a sense of proportion about these distinctions. We do not need to grovel before the stars and the billionaires. If this is what is meant by egalitarianism, then I trust that all of us are egalitarians, and we would not want it any other way. Yet that is compatible with practically any degree and kind of real inequality that you can imagine. Some people are brilliant, most are not; some are beautiful, most are not; some are swift, most are not; and so on, without end. We can, and we should, acknowledge this without resentment.

If it bothers you that somebody is better than you are at something, you can either try to improve yourself, or try to bring down the person in question. The general right of liberty forbids doing the latter: if that is how you feel, too bad for you—you will just have to live it. Nature provides people with a vast array of differences, many of which do not matter and some of which do. But it is no fault of the people on the perceived upper end of any of these comparisons that they are there, and in many cases it is a virtue, for they often get there by dint of tremendously hard work, concentration, and discipline, in addition to inborn talent.

Some egalitarians talk as though this should be a matter of terrible concern—as though the gods have done an awful thing there, and we humans must do our best to level out the differences. True, most egalitarians do not explicitly say that, though it is not entirely clear why not; they largely avoid or talk around these things. But to them, I think we should say, "Get real!" For in truth, people who are terrific at all sorts of different things are a benefit to us all, not a cause for resentment, hand-wringing, or affirmative action programs. The better any of our fellows are at anything useful to anyone and harmful to no one, the better. But the idea that in order to bring it about that this person is better at something we should actually force other people to contribute their help simply does not go. Those who like to help are welcome to help; those who do not are welcome not to.

Let's start with the rich, who are so widely deplored by so many theorists. The rich who have got rich in business or sports or the arts, which comprises almost all of them, have got there by doing us all favors. You get rich in business only if a lot of people buy your products, and they will only do that if they find them worth buying—worth buying again and again, for that matter. Well, how can this be bad? All those customers think themselves better off for those purchases, and they are usually right. It is business people who have enabled them to be so. That is a good thing, not a bad one.

Again, consider the Beautiful People. Most of us are so-so, though many do their best to be better than that. But is not the sight of a beautiful woman (I'm a man, so I list them first!) or a handsome man a pleasure to the eye? Or someone dressed in a fabulous gown? In any case, do we really want everyone to look the same? Am I not better off living in a society in which there are many people who are more attractive than I, richer than I, better at all sorts of things than I? Indeed I am. I am grateful to all these people for being around, and of course for all the nice things— great musical or athletic performances, pleasant sights in restaurants, streets, or on the TV screen—that they provide us. Surely the attitude that condemns all this richness is one to deplore. Indeed, it can only be antihuman, at bottom, to condemn such things, for what are humans if not, above all, different from each other? To deplore this can only be to demean humanity.

CONCLUSION

At the outset, I suggested that the question of proportions between liberty and equality sounded somewhat biased against extreme answers. But in the end, we are left with what some will no doubt claim to be an extreme answer. The primary question we are concerned with is, concerning liberty and equality, how much of each do we get to enforce? And to that question, my answer is, we get to enforce liberty, as a general right, but insofar as the equality of anything else is in question, as such, it has no claims whatever. Once we see the distinction between universal rights and egalitarian rights, we will, I think, see the wisdom of accepting universal rights to liberty and rejecting universal rights to enforced equalities. Comparing liberty and equality, liberty wins.

CHAPTER THREE

An Unladylike Meditation on Egalitarianism

Ellen R. Klein

Refraining mutually from injury, violence, and exploitation and placing one's will on a par with that of someone else—this may become, in a certain rough sense, good manners among individuals if the appropriate conditions are present. . . . But as soon as this principle is extended, and possibly even accepted as the fundamental principle of society, *it immediately proves to be what it really is—a will to the* denial *of life, a principle of disintegration and decay.*

—Friedrich Nietzsche[1]

IF TODAY'S SAVVY contemporary feminist could attain the equality she desires from the "male" known as American society, what would such sociopolitical changes entail? This is one of the questions that keeps me, a self-proclaimed antifeminist, up at night.

One would think that, for a woman, the prospect of winning

I am playing on Nietzsche's title *Untimely Meditations*, which was the inspiration for this piece. (Nietzsche's text can be viewed as "untimely" in several ways: "[Nietzsche is an 'untimely' writer for] he writes as one who is well-acquainted and imbued with the spirit of Greek antiquity. . . . his perspective on the present is 'untimely' precisely because of his urgent concern with the future. . . . [the 'untimeliness' of the essays are] a necessary consequence of striving to become who one is." Daniel Breazeale, ed., *Nietzsche's Untimely Meditations* (Cambridge: Cambridge University Press, 1999), pp. xlvi–xlvii.

1. Friedrich Nietzsche, *Beyond Good and Evil: Prelude to a Philosophy of the Future*, trans. Walter Kaufman (New York: Vintage Books, 1966), p. 259.

every feminist battle in the classroom, the boardroom, or the court-room would be nothing less than comforting, if not downright exciting. But precisely the opposite is true. I'm terrified. Contemporary feminism has, to date, done its job so precisely wrongly in so many ways concerning so many different venues, and their handling of sociopolitical questions concerning egalitarianism is simply one more example.

No "ism," I will now argue, has made a mockery of our society's commitment to freedom, individualism, and liberty more than feminism. Like all good liberals, feminists have discussed the previously mentioned sociopolitical issues while assuming that it is equality, not liberty, that is the essence of justice in our society. Whether this is true or false, is, of course, the heart of the debate between the egalitarian and the libertarian.

Traditionally, on one side of the egalitarianism spectrum is the ambiguous, and therefore innocuous, dictionary definition that claims simply that an egalitarian is one who believes that "all men are equal" without defining either who is a man or what it means to be equal. At the other end is the unambiguous but little-ad-hered-to belief in what can be characterized as the old left. "The idea that genuine equality among citizens holds only when every-one has the same wealth, cradle to grave, no matter whether he chooses to work or what work he chooses . . . and that it is the proper role of government to ensure that everyone has the same wealth no matter what."[2] Of course, it is somewhere in the middle where the interesting philosophical,[3] political,[4] and economic[5] work is being done.

2. Ronald Dworkin, *Sovereign Virtue: The Theory and Practice of Equality* (Cambridge: Harvard University Press, 2000), p. 2.

3. For example, Richard J. Arneson, "Egalitarianism and Responsibility," *The Journal of Ethics* 3 (1999): 225–47; Mark A. Michael, "Environmental Egalitarianism and 'Who do you Save?'," *Environmental Values* 6 (1997): 307–25;

Both sides seem to be struggling with how to balance the two fundamental components of justice—equality and liberty. Many libertarians recognize that, to some degree or other, equity is at least a part of liberty;[6] and the egalitarian seems to have no choice but to admit that "we can secure Equality in certain respects between members of certain classes for certain purposes and under certain conditions; but never, and necessarily never, Equality in all respects between all men or all purposes and under all conditions."[7] But what passes as feminist theorizing concerning the important debate not only neglects to finesse some middle ground but also it is not even in the proverbial ballpark. That is, whatever it is that contemporary feminists are doing when they claim to be discussing equality, is so problematic (on so many different levels) that they must be considered to be even beyond left field.

Although it may be the case that an egalitarian interested in some kind of absolute equality is "doomed to a life not only of grumbling

---

Norman P. Barry, "The Philosophy of the Welfare State," *Critical Review* (Fall 1990): 545–68.

4. For example, Andrew Levine, "Rewarding Effort," *The Journal of Political Philosophy* 7, no. 4 (1999): 404–18; Ken Binmore, "Egalitarianism versus Utilitarianism" *Utilitas* 10, no. 3 (November 1998): 353–67; John Christman, "Self-Ownership, Equality, and the Structure of Property Rights," *Political Theory* 19, no. 1 (February 1991): 28–46.

5. For example, Robert William Fogel, *The Fourth Great Awakening and the Future of Egalitarianism* (Chicago: University Chicago Press, 2000); Samuel Bowles and Herbert Gintis, *Recasting Egalitarianism: New Rules for Communities, States and Markets*, vol. 3, *The Real Utopias Project*, ed. Erik Olin Wright (London & New York: Verso, 1998).

6. See, for example, Thomas W. Platt, "Chance, Equity, and Social Justice," in Yaeger Hudson, ed., *Rending and Renewing the Social Order* (Lewiston, N.Y.: Edwin Mellen Press, 1996), pp. 277–86.

7. J. L. Lucas, "Equality," in Richard E. Flathman, ed., *Concepts in Social and Political Philosophy* (New York: Macmillan, 1973), p. 351. In Louis Pojman, "Equality: A Plethora of Theories," *Journal of Philosophical Research* 24 (1999): 193–245, this is called "absolute equality," and it is made obvious that given the contingencies of the universe that this kind of ideal is "impossible" (pp. 205–6).

and everlasting envy, of endless and inevitable disappointment,"[8] the feminist egalitarian ends up extricating herself from the debate altogether. Her notion of equality is nothing less than unreasonable because, unlike nonfeminist egalitarians, it does not suffer from the traditional problem of trying to go "beyond an assertion of similarity to an assertion of identity,"[9] but precisely the opposite. Feminism not only tries to force the concept of equality into meaning difference, but does so while attempting to show how the goal of justice is itself a male-constructed and -biased notion. She not only does not want to play by the rules, she wants the rules to change to meet her political goals, or else she threatens simply to take her ball and go home.

Therefore, in what follows, I will argue that it is responsible to view feminist theories of equality as being, at best, an intellectual exercise that is part of an entirely different game; at worst, such theorizing is simply a pernicious attempt to create a notion of justice that not only avoids all personal responsibility but also actually curtails liberties. This emasculating of the American mind is not only obviously harmful to society as a whole, it has the ironic and very unfeminist effect of harming women in particular.[10] As such, no version of feminist egalitarianism[11] should be taken to be even a

8. J. L. Lucas, "Equality," p. 351.
9. Geoffrey Cupit, "The Basis of Equity," *Philosophy* 75 (2000): 111.
10. See my forthcoming book, *The Emasculating of the American Mind: How Feminism Has Enabled Mediocrity.*
11. I say no version because feminist theorists (in all areas) love to become a moving target. They do this first by insisting that there is no such thing as "feminism," only feminism*s*, and secondly by denying that even the desire to search for some kind of coalescing foundation is fundamentally sexist. Nonetheless, many of their ranks claim that "although feminists may have disparate values, we share the same goal of equality." (Jennifer Baumgardner and Amy Richards, *Manifesta: Young Women, Feminism, and the Future* [New York: Farrar, Straus, and Giroux, 2000], p. 280) At the very least it seems one has at least a prima facie right to attempt to distill whatever is peculiarly feminist from their so-called feminist accounts of egalitarianism and equality.

serious contender among the variety of egalitarian theories,[12] let alone given further opportunities to affect moral and/or legal policy making in the United States.

HISTORY

> *In all the countries of Europe, and in America, too, there now is some-thing that abuses this name. . . . they belong, briefly and sadly, among the* levelers—*these falsely so-called "free spirits"—being eloquent and prolifically scribbling slaves of the democratic taste and its 'modern ideas' . . . only they are unfree and ridiculously superficial, above all in their basic inclination to find in the forms of the old society as it has existed so far just about the cause of all human misery and failure—which is a way of standing truth happily upon her head! What they would like to strive for with all their powers is the universal green-pasture happiness of the herd, with security, lack of danger, comfort, and an easier life for everyone; the two songs and doctrines they repeat most often are "equality of rights" and "sympathy for all sufferers."*
>
> —Friedrich Nietzsche[13]

The classical (Western) history of the ideal of equality begins with the Old Testament, the first five books containing the story of a people chosen, picked out to be unequal. The later Psalms and Proverbs go on to make yet further distinctions, namely, between the good and the bad person. Plato too believed it most important to recognize difference (with respect to degrees of human excel-lence) rather than similarity between individuals. Thus, his "formal"[14] maxim of equality, which was later stated directly by Aristotle, was simply, "Equals are to be treated equally and unequals unequally. . . . Injustice arises when equals are treated unequally and also when unequals are treated equally."[15]

---

12. Louis Pojman categorizes eighteen fundamentally different forms of egal-itarianism. See Pojman, "Equality."

13. Friedrich Nietzsche, *Beyond Good and Evil*, p. 44.

14. So called, for example, by Pojman, "Equality," pp. 195–98.

15. Aristotle, *Nichomachean Ethics*, Book V.

With the New Testament, an interesting distinction between man judging man simpliciter and man being judged via the eyes of God[16] is first developed. In Galatians 3–4, it is claimed that everyone who chooses Christ is chosen; and in Corinthians 8:13–14, the first seeds of communism are sown: "Our desire is not that others might be relieved while you are hard pressed, but that there might be equality. At the present time your plenty will supply what they need, so that in turn their plenty will supply what you need."[17]

"Modern egalitarianism had its beginnings in the seventeenth century with the Calvinist doctrine that although there is a sharp difference between the damned and the saved, there is no difference between the clergy and the lay community of the faithful."[18] And the modern political philosophers—for example, Hobbes, Locke, and Rousseau—took it from there.

For Hobbes, all people come into the world selfish, brutish, and in constant danger. There is no question that everyone is basically equally susceptible to the hardships of the environment and the needs and desires of others born into the same plight. The question of political equality took the form of something very simple, the right to individual self-preservation, which later was developed into the right of the sovereign to protect his or her nation and people at all costs. Peace, for Hobbes, overrode equity as the ultimate good.

Locke, though similar to Hobbes in a number of respects, had a more sophisticated view of rights and argued that the community must always retain the power to overthrow government if "legislators ever become so foolish or wicked as to lay and carry designs

16. Pojman calls this "metaphysical equality" because "all humans are of equal and positive value before God," "Equality," pp. 195–98. Nietzsche has an interesting view on this notion: "They fight for the 'equality of all men before God' and almost *need* faith in God just for that," *Beyond Good and Evil*, p. 219.

17. Pojman calls this "metaphysical equality" because "all humans are of equal and positive value before God," "Equality," p. 219.

18. Stanley I. Benn, "Equality, Moral and Social," in *The Encyclopedia of Philosophy*, vols. 3 and 4 (New York: Macmillan, 1967), pp. 38–42.

against their liberties and properties."[19] What counts for Locke as "designs" against such "liberties and properties," especially with respect to government intervention, remains undeveloped.

Rousseau, however, changed all that. His optimistic view of human beings sees them in a garden and not in the Hobbesian jungle. As such, many of the problems that befall humans, both as separate individuals and as a collective, are the fault of society itself. "Man is born free; and everywhere is in chains."[20] Here we see that the first rumblings of the change in blame and therefore responsibility—from the individual to society.

The year now is 1776 and the Founding Fathers have just drafted the Declaration of Independence claiming that "all men are created equal . . . endowed by their creator with certain unalienable rights . . . life, liberty, and the pursuit of happiness." A few years later this is joined by the Constitution with its claims to "create a more perfect Union, establish Justice, insure domestic Tranquility, provide for the common Defence, promote the general Welfare, and secure the Blessings of Liberty to ourselves and our Posterity." With the spirit of elasticity backed up by ambiguous language, equity becomes a notion of equal under the law of the land, but the actual role of government in helping individuals achieve their own personal pursuits of happiness, as well as our general pursuits of welfare, is left indeterminate.

Some interpretation of government's role is given in *The Federalist Papers*[21] although the original Constitution guarantees very few rights. One is our right to national security (both from foreign and

---

19. John Locke, *Second Treatise on Government*, edited by C. B. Macpherson (Indianapolis, Ind.: Hackett, 1980), pp. 77–78, sect. 149.

20. Jean-Jacques Rousseau, "Social Contract," in *The Social Contract and Discourses*, trans. G. B. H. Cole (New York: J. M. Dent and Sons, 1973).

21. For example, Madison's "The Federalist No. 41," in Alexander Hamilton, John Jay, and James Madison, eds., *The Federalist: A Commentary on the Constitution of the United States* (New York: Random House, 1941), pp. 259–270; see especially p. 261.

domestic enemies), another is a concomitant commitment to economic prosperity (in order that one can tax the people to fund such security). Even a commitment to the education of the masses is not directly addressed because at the time a primarily agrarian market needed nothing more than strong bodies to defend the Union efficaciously.

It was not until the advent of the abolition of slavery that a more positive account of equality under the law was created, which grew into what we now call legal equality, though the language remains negative.[22] The Thirteenth Amendment (1865) makes slavery illegal, the Fourteenth Amendment (1868) outlines due process, and the Fifteenth (1870) ensures that all men have the right to vote. Nonetheless, all of these precepts are couched in a language of "shall nots." The point is simple: all three of these pre–civil rights[23] amendments attempt to ensure that no rights (interpreted as rights already granted elsewhere in the Constitution) are to be taken away from any group of men, not that any privilege is added.

So how did the myriad of the contemporary varieties of egalitarianism evolve from this minimalist construct of legal equality? Marx?

Assuming this would be very problematic. For one thing, it is not clear that anything like an account of equality at all, let alone the sophisticated and nuanced accounts that have become popular in the contemporary literature, can be considered truly Marxist. Given that the primary rallying point of Marxist theorizing has always been "from each according to his ability; to each according

22. Pojman claims that the construct of "legal equality" is simply redundant because what else could "equality" mean if not "equality under the law . . . giving the false appearance that equality is a separate and independent norm." Pojman, "Equality," pp. 201–203.

23. I call them pre–civil rights since it was not until the poll tax was removed in 1964, by the Twenty-Fourth Amendment, that true civil rights actually began.

to his need,"[24] it is more likely that one person with no ability (albeit with extravagant needs) would end up with goods that were seriously unequal to those from whom such goods and/or services arose.[25]

No, it must have been something simply in the zeitgeist of the American mind itself. The unique, hopeful, and to a great extent luxurious, frontier that was the United States had a mind all its own, and that mind was set on valuing equity (though one important commentator of American life at the time, Alexis de Tocqueville, is quite hard pressed to discover why). In a chapter of *Democracy in America* entitled "Why Democratic Nations Show a More Ardent and Enduring Love of Equality Than of Liberty," de Tocqueville states,

> Freedom has appeared in the world at different times and under various forms; it has not been exclusively bound to any social condition, and it is not confined to democracies. Freedom cannot, therefore, form the distinguishing characteristic of democratic ages. The peculiar and preponderant fact that marks those ages as its own is the equality of condition; the ruling passion of men in those periods is the love of this equality. Do not ask what singular charm the men of democratic ages find in being equal, or what special reasons they may have for clinging so tenaciously to equality rather than to the other advantages that society holds out to them: equality is the distinguishing characteristic of the age they live in; that of itself is enough to explain that they prefer it to all the rest.[26]

24. Karl Marx, "Critique of the Gotha Programme," *Karl Marx and Friedrich Engels: Reader*, (ed.) Robert C. Tucker (New York: W. W. Norton and Co., 1978), pp. 525–41.

25. Dworkin does a great job avoiding this kind of criticism by emphasizing that there is a huge difference between "Marxist" and egalitarian goals when he states that his notion of equality clearly distinguishes between creating "a nation of equals and a nation of addicts." Dworkin, *Sovereign Virtue*, p. 303.

26. Alexis de Tocqueville, *Democracy in America* (New York: Alfred A. Knopf, 1972), p. 95.

Though most of his work is purely descriptive, he does add a warning to those who hold such a value:

> The evils that freedom sometimes brings with it are immediate; they are apparent to all, and all are more or less affected by them. The evils that extreme equality may produce are slowly disclosed; they creep gradually into the social frame; they are seen only at intervals; and at the moment at which they become most violent, habit already causes them to be no longer felt.[27]

Drunk on equity, however, America was not. There was still one major group of people who remained, even legally, unequal. It was not until 1920 that the Nineteenth Amendment was passed and, again in negative language, stated that "the rights of citizens to vote shall not be denied or abridged by the United States or by any State on account of sex."

However, although the story of equality for women begins here, *feminist egalitarianism* does not. What Wollstonecraft and others argued for, what was eventually acknowledged via the Constitution, was that women are full citizens.[28] Women were no longer to be seen as fundamentally distinct from, nor inferior to, men because the most significant gender differences in intellectual skills, temperament, and ethical values were argued to be merely products of socialization and education, rather than biological facts. Her modest claim was simply that "in the absence of comparative data based on egalitarian learning environments from earliest childhood, maintaining that men and women are intellectually and morally different can only reflect irrational prejudice."[29]

And many men, as well as first-generation feminists, agreed with

27. De Tocqueville, *Democracy in America*, p. 96.

28. Mary Wollstonecraft, *A Vindication of the Rights of Women*, ed. Carl H. Poston (1792; Reprint, New York: W. W. Norton, 1975).

29. Eve Cole Browning, *Philosophy and Feminist Criticism: An Introduction* (New York: Paragon House, 1993), pp. 3–4.

this finding.[30] At the very least the consensus today seems to be that the well educated from both sides of the sexual divide claim that "the arguments against women's equality have been illogical and have had little legitimate claim to be based on known biological facts."[31] Or, even more modestly, that "the biological and statistical bases for upholding either dogma are absent."[32] If this is true, then certainly women were at least deserving of the most minimal interpretation of legal equality, that is, the right to vote.[33]

However, the right to vote was not enough. Feminists demanded more and for some pretty good reasons. First, as Mill pointed out years before, it seems pragmatically silly to maintain any sanctions prohibiting women from acquiring equal opportunity with respect to education or employment because "what women by nature cannot do, it is quite superfluous to forbid them from doing; what they can do but not so well as the men who are their competitors, competition suffices to exclude them . . ."[34] However the dismantling of social sanctions against women quickly turned

30. It is important to distinguish what I have elsewhere called "first-generation feminism" (old-time feminism focusing on equal opportunity and equal pay), "second-generation feminism" (prevalent in contemporary academia, where feminists are more interested in the destruction of everything male, especially the philosophical underpinnings of science and ethics), and "third generation feminism" (which I hope will "go back to the future" [see, e.g., Klein, *Feminism under Fire* (Amherst, N.Y.: Prometheus, 1996)] and rekindle what was important in the first generation) from what is now called first-, second-, and third-wave feminisms cited elsewhere.

31. Gisela T. Kaplan and Lesley J. Rogers, "The Definition of Male and Female: Biological Reductionism and the Sanctions of Normality," in Sneja Gunew, ed., *Feminist Knowledge: Critique and Construct* (New York: Routledge, 1990), p. 206.

32. Tibor Machan, *Liberty and Culture: Essays on the Idea of a Free Society.* (Buffalo: Prometheus, 1989), p. 257.

33. Actually this biological "fact" is still being debated. See, e.g., Michael Levin, "Maritime Policy for a Flat Earth," in James Sterba, ed., *Controversies in Feminism* (New York: Rowman and Littlefield, 2001), pp. 197–223.

34. John Stuart Mill, *The Subjection of Women*, ed. Sue Mansfield (Arlington Heights, Ill.: Harlan Davidson, 1980), p. 26.

into assuming that something more than legal equality—the limited egalitarianism established by the Declaration of Independence (i.e., life, liberty, and the pursuit of happiness), combined with the Nineteenth Amendment—should actually be protected by government.

And this brings us to the second reason feminists were capable of generating sympathy for what has developed into a ridiculous, if not pernicious, political agenda: timing. Given that the American mind seems to bias equality, as opposed to liberty, as being the more basic principle of justice, a richer notion of equality had finally become status quo.[35] With the left gaining power, a fuller egalitarianism of some form or other soon became the norm. Feminism, as a branch of liberalism, Marxism, and/or socialism, simply reaped the benefit of being at the right place at the right time. With equality now holding a privileged position, what was still up for grabs was only what counted as equal in the minds of the contemporary feminist.[36]

Though the Equal Rights Amendment[37] was beginning to make

---

35. To read an opposing viewpoint, see the wonderful collection of essays by Tibor Machan in *Liberty and Culture.*

36. This presupposition is brought into question by certain theorists, e.g., G. A. Cohen, "The Pareto Argument for Inequality," in Ellen Frankel, Fred D. Miller, Jr., and Jeffrey Paul, eds., *Contemporary Political and Social Philosophy* (Cambridge: Cambridge University Press, 1995), p. 163. See also Patrick Shaw, "The Pareto Argument and Inequality," *The Philosophical Quarterly* 49, no. 196 (July 1999): 353–68.

37. The political push for the ERA began in 1972 and ended in 1982. It was intended to "constitutionally guarantee women equality under the law," the spirit being that the burden of proof would switch from individual women having to prove they were discriminated against, to the institutionalized power (specifically government) having to show that they are not discriminating. Case law, soon after, ended up making a de facto commitment to the ERA when in *Craig v. Boren*, 429 U.S. 190, in 1976, the government was barred from relying on gender classifications unless they served important governmental objectives and were substantially related to the achievement of those objectives. This law has set the precedent for keeping women out of only a small and select area of military service, specifically serving as a submariner or a Navy Seal (Bureau of Navy Personnel).

waves, few operational ideas concerning egalitarianism in general had been seriously expressed (and few articles[38] and books were published) until Rawls wrote *A Theory of Justice*.[39] That was when the floodgates of theorizing opened on campuses across the country concerning egalitarianism, though the specific question of women was still not being directly addressed. Generally speaking, then, although it is clear that egalitarian theories of justice hold that some version of equality should be promoted, even if perfect equality is probably impossible to achieve, the practical question becomes one of what is the best form of equality we can achieve just short of perfection.[40]

According to Stanley Benn, for example, "there are three ways of ascribing equality—descriptive, evaluative, and distributive—and they are not, of course independent of one another."[41] And the more contemporary theorist Louis P. Pojman has since documented eighteen distinct kinds of egalitarianism[42] (each with as many subcategories as there are authors). To both the gross and detailed breakdowns is added feminist egalitarianism.

As is the case with all areas of feminist construction to date, it must be at least compared to, if not built from, the male and, therefore according to such theorists, the "fundamentally sexist and

38. One notable exception in the legal field is Herbert Wechsler, "Toward Neutral Principles of Constitutional Law," *Columbia Law Review* 73, issue 1, (1959): 11–15. One notable exception in the philosophical field is Herbert Marcuse in his essay "Repressive Tolerance," in Robert P. Wolff, Barrington Moore Jr., and Herbert Marcuse, eds., *A Critique of Pure Tolerance* (Boston: Beacon Press, 1965), pp. 81–123.

39. John Rawls, *A Theory of Justice* (Cambridge: Harvard University Press, 1971).

40. See, e.g., Peter Valentine, "Equality, Efficiency, and the Priority of the Worse-Off," *Economics and Philosophy* 16 (2000): 1–19.

41. Stanley I. Benn, "Egalitarianism and the Equal Consideration of Interests," in Richard E. Flathman, ed., *Concepts in Social and Political Philosophy* (New York: Macmillan, 1973), p. 337.

42. Pojman, "Equality," pp. 201–3.

oppressive" theory that sparked its development.[43] What will be demonstrated is the impotence of such theorizing in making any progress toward a viable notion of what it means to be equal. I will show that those "feminist" accounts of equity that are plausible are not particularly feminist; those that are truly feminist are fundamentally inconsistent with any reasonable notion of equality.

HERSTORY

Women can, through a few centuries of education, be made into anything, even into men: not in the sexual sense, to be sure, but in every other sense. Under such a regimen they will one day have acquired all the male strengths and virtues, though they will also of course have had to accept all their weaknesses and vices in the bargain: thus much can, as aforesaid, be extorted. But how shall we endure the intermediate stage, which may itself last a couple of centuries, during which the primeval properties of women, their follies and injustices, are still asserting themselves over what has been newly learned and acquired?

—Friedrich Nietzsche[44]

We begin then with Rawls, who claims that justice is the establishing of rules that allow one to resolve conflicts through "political procedures that are reasonably regarded as fair."[45] And fairness in turn is prescribed by a commitment to the following notion of equality:

Some writers have distinguished between equality as it is invoked in connection with the distribution of certain goods, some of which will almost certainly give higher status or prestige to those who are more favored, and equality as it applied to respect which is owed to persons irrespective of their social position. Equality of the first kind

43. See, e.g., Klein, *Feminism under Fire.*
44. Friedrich Nietzsche, *Human, All Too Human: A Book for Free Spirits*, trans. Hollingdale (Cambridge: Cambridge University Press, 1996), Part I, p. 425.
45. Rawls, *A Theory of Justice*, p. 356.

is defined by the second principle of justice. . . . But equality of the second kind is fundamental.[46]

And although the years of scholarship that have passed since its publication have created a plethora of interpretations and commentary on Rawls's theory, some have stood the test of time as having captured the essence of Rawls.

For example, one contemporary of Rawls claimed that

> Rawls lays it down that a practice is just if everyone is treated alike, unless a discrimination in favor of some is of advantage to everyone. We can now translate this into the language of equal interests: If all basic interests are already being satisfied and if there is no universally acknowledged order of priority as between further interest competing for satisfaction, then, given that the individual has a fundamental interest in determining what are his own interests, a practice would be just that gave all interests actually competing in a situation equal satisfaction, save insofar as an inequality made possible a greater degree of satisfaction without weakening claims that would be satisfied without it.[47]

Basically, in the final analysis, Rawls was arguing for what has become his now famous thesis: "justice as fairness." "The hope for social institutions that do not confer morally arbitrary lifelong advantages on some persons at the expense of others."[48]

A number of theorists oppose Rawls's principle for several different reasons, for example, the substantive reason that Rawls's account only discusses the equality of opportunity at what Dworkin calls the "starting-gate" without due concern for the overall achievement of equal opportunity of outcomes.[49] But what bothers feminists is much more problematic. After all, "feminism is essen-

46. Rawls, *A Theory of Justice*, p. 511.

47. Benn, "Egalitarianism and the Equal Consideration of Interests," p. 347.

48. Thomas Nagel, "Rawls, John," in Ted Honderich, ed., *The Oxford Companion to Philosophy* (New York: Oxford University Press, 1995), pp. 745–46.

49. Dworkin, *Sovereign Virtue*, p. 87.

tially concerned with the elimination of a certain *type* of injustice."[50] What type they are after, however, is more than a little unclear.

Feminist theorists, for example, claim that the problem with Rawls's account is that

> Although Rawls says that each party to the original position must agree with all the rest on which available alternative is the best conception of justice, in fact that agreement is otiose because each party in his original position follows the same reasoning procedure and reaches the same conclusion—namely, that the Rawlsian conception of justice is preferable to all others. . . . And this shows that it isn't the contract device that is the substance of his theory but the conception of worth that informs the device. . . . I do not regard Rawls' contract test as a morally neutral device . . . since it could be successfully used to disallow the commodization of a womb.[51]

But what is still left unclear is just what is offensive.

The issue of what it actually means to view the womb as a commodity aside, one must first wonder if the problem with the "contract test" is simply that it places oneself "in the original position" behind the "veil of ignorance" without enabling one to imagine oneself pregnant? If so, this seems to be simply false. The "veil" prevents nothing of the kind. On the contrary it seems to allow for precisely this kind of shoe-fitting.

Is it that in order for the contract test to be viewed as morally neutral with respect to women, one has actually to imagine oneself as a woman? Again, there seems to be no fundamentally psychological problem with such an imagining unless, of course, there is some biological reason why a man, for example, could not imagine him-

50. Moira Gatens, *Feminism and Philosophy: Perspectives on Difference and Equality* (Bloomington: Indiana University Press, 1991), p. 90.

51. Jean Hampton, "Feminist Contractarianism," in Louise M. Antony and Charlotte Witt, eds., *A Mind of One's Own: Feminist Essays on Reason and Objectivity* (Boulder: Westview Press, 1993), pp. 227–55.

self in someone else's pumps. Maybe the point is simply that even if a man imagined himself fully female, and fully impregnatable (or even fully pregnant), he would be incapable of appropriately valuing that status in socioeconomic terms. All such concerns, of course, presuppose not only that no women would be in the "original position" but that even if the "position" were all male, such beings would, by the very fact of their maleness, act in ways that are prima facie unjust. Such moves seem not only unfair to Rawls but essentially sexist.

Maybe the problem is more fundamental. Maybe it is that Rawls's theory is too contractarian and not utilitarian enough. This is one of the criticisms raised by, for example, Tom Regan.

> The great appeal of utilitarianism rests with its uncompromising egalitarianism: everyone's interests count and count as much as the like interests of everyone else. The kind of odious discrimination that some forms of contractarianism can justify—discrimination based on race or sex, for example—seems disallowed in principle by utilitarianism, as is speciesism, the systematic discrimination based on species membership.[52]

The problematic fact that human beings are such a fundamentally different and discernible species from all other species aside, there is a more interesting problem concerning the question of the kinds of species that can even have rights and liberties and be in need of what Robert Nozick calls "moral space."[53]

On the other hand, it may be that Rawls' account is too utilitar-

---

52. Tom Regan, "The Case for Animal Rights," in Peter Singer, ed., *In Defense of Animals* (Oxford: Blackwell, 1985), pp. 13–26, reprinted in James E. White, ed., *Contemporary Moral Problems* (New York: Wadsworth, 2000), p. 504.

53. For a provocative analysis of the rights of animals and interesting discussion of applications of rights and liberties to other species (which is outside the scope of this paper) see, e.g., Tibor R. Machan, "Do Animals Have Rights?" in White, ed., *Contemporary Moral Problems*, pp. 509–15.

ian and not contractarian enough.[54] After all, at bottom, Rawls's theory emphasizes a form of objective social commitment that is not "situated" or relativized enough to the woman's "standpoint."[55] Feminist theorists have traditionally, at least since Gilligan, valued the contextual while vilifying the universal.[56]

To be fair, it may be that Rawls is simply too Hobbesian. This would also be a problem for the feminist theorist given that Hobbes, like any other man who is part of the patriarchal sociopolitical and philosophical structure, portrays in his theorizing a pretense that is typical of such dominant moral theories and traditions. What is typical (and "typical" is to be seen as a serious admonition) is that theories such as Hobbes's are interested in discussing the relationships between moral equals such as those who would be considered in the "original position." However, this desire, according to feminism, is a pretense, because there is no equality to be had for a woman when the contract must be made with a man—the "pretense of an equality that is, in fact, absent."[57]

Nor did actual operational effects of feminism hold any weight. By 1976, *Craig v. Boren* had been litigated and law was created that made it explicit that the "government was barred from relying on gender classifications unless they served important government objectives and were substantially related to the achievement of those objectives."[58] Nonetheless women remained suspicious about the

54. See, e.g., Virginia Held, "Caring Relations and Principles of Justice," in James Sterba, ed., *Controversies in Feminism* (New York: Rowman and Littlefield, 2001), p. 79.

55. A word coined by Sandra Harding. See, e.g., *The Science Question in Feminism* (Ithaca: Cornell University Press, 1986).

56. Carol Gilligan, *In a Different Voice* (Cambridge: Harvard University Press, 1982). For a critique of this valuing, see E. R. Klein, "Criticizing the Feminist Critique of Objectivity," *Reason Papers* 18 (1993): 57–70.

57. Annette Baier, "The Need for More Justice," in Marsha Hanen and Kair Nielsen, eds., *Science, Morality, and Feminist Theory* (Calgary: University of Calgary Press, 1987), p. 52.

58. *Craig v. Boren*, 429 U.S. 190, 1976.

law and the male construct of equity under which it was formulated.

> I am afraid that old women are more skeptical in their most secret heart of hearts than any man: they consider the superficiality of existence its essence, and all virtue and profundity is to them merely a veil over this 'truth,' a very welcome veil over a pudendum—in other words, a matter of decency and shame, no more than that.[59]

Were feminists being overly cautious by attempting to pass the ERA, or were they correct that such case law was merely a red herring, another piece of evidence that male contemporary culture was simply feigning equity? Furthermore, was this supposed problem of the feigned notion of equality peculiar to duty-based theories such as Rawls's, or was it endemic to egalitarian theories in general? What of, for example, the rights-based egalitarianism of someone like Dworkin? According to Dworkin:

> There are two different sorts of rights one may be said to have. The first is the right to equal treatment, which is the right to an equal distribution of some opportunity or resource or burden. Every citizen, for example, has a right to an equal vote in a democracy; that is the nerve of the Supreme Court's decision that one person must have one vote even if a different and more complex arrangement would better secure the collective welfare. The second is the right to treatment as an equal, which is the right not to receive the same distribution of some burden or benefit, but to be treated with the same respect and concern as anyone else. If I have two children, and one is dying from a disease that is making the other uncomfortable, I do not show equal concern if I flip a coin to decide which should have the remaining dose of a drug. This example shows that the right to treatment as an equal is fundamental, and the right to equal treatment, derivative. . . . I propose that the right to treatment as an

59. Friedrich Nietzsche, *The Gay Science*, trans. Walter Kaufman (New York: Vintage Books, 1974), p. 64.

equal must be taken to be fundamental under the liberal conception of equality.[60]

Here, too, however, feminists take umbrage. For even the modest rights talk is seen as fundamentally sexist.

Carole Pateman, for example, claims that when feminist egalitarianism is taken to be "nothing more than equality in the sense of women attaining the same status as individuals, workers, or citizens, as men, it is difficult to find a convincing defense against the long-standing anti-feminist charge that such theorists want to turn women into men."[61] Despite the fact that it may simply be an empirical point that "Americans are wedded to individualism—the idea that each person is sovereign in his own life,"[62] feminists think such an attitude is fundamentally sexist. Stressing the Cartesian "I" essential to all individualism, according to many feminists, ignores the body and, therefore, is essentially sexist.[63] In other words, feminist egalitarianism cannot be achieved until notions of equality recognize the "political significance of women's bodies, to press for the inclusion of 'women as women' rather than as equals to men."[64]

Let us take stock here for a second, because I am sure you think I must be grossly misunderstanding the feminist account of egalitarianism, given that egalitarianism simpliciter is about equality, and

60. Ronald Dworkin, *Taking Rights Seriously* (Cambridge: Harvard University Press, 1978), pp. 227 and 272.

61. Carole Pateman, "Introduction," in Carole Pateman and Elizabeth Gross, eds., *Feminist Challenges: Social and Political Theory* (Boston: Northeastern University Press, 1987), pp. 7–8.

62. Tibor Machan, "Utopian Americans and False Guilt About the Poor," in Machan, *Liberty and Culture*, p. 274.

63. See, e.g., Lorraine Code, *What Can She Know? Feminist Theory and the Construction of Knowledge* (Ithaca: Cornell University Press, 1991), p. 5. See also Rosie Bradotti, "Feminism and Modernity," *Free Inquiry* 15, no. 2 (Spring 1995): 24–28.

64. Susan Moller Okin, "Feminism and Political Theory," in Janet Kourany, ed., *Philosophy in a Feminist Voice* (Princeton: Princeton University Press, 1998), p. 123.

yet the feminist theorists above seem to be arguing for something that sounds like inequality. This is because they do not want to discuss equality, at least not until there is a radical rethinking of the nature of equality.

The queen of this doublespeak is Catherine MacKinnon. MacKinnon claims that looking at the notion of equality as the foundation for a feminist egalitarianism will not be fruitful because women cannot be equal citizens until there is a radical rethinking of the public and domestic sphere of life and the relationship between the two. For MacKinnon, every relationship with a man—from private sex to public office—is so infused with male bias that there would be no way even to understand the construct of equality under such patriarchy:

> Virtually every quality that distinguished men from women is already affirmatively compensated in this society. Men's physiology defines most sports, their needs define auto and health coverage, their socially designed biographies define workplace expectations and successful career patterns, their perspectives and concerns define quality in scholarship, their experiences and obsessions define merit, their objectification of life defines art, their military service defines citizenship, their presence defines family, their inability to get along with each other—their wars and rulerships—define history, their image defines god, and their genitals define sex. For each of their differences from women, what amounts to an affirmative action plan is in effect, otherwise known as the structure and values of American society.[65]

What she wants is for the "state to abandon its pose of neutrality, which [she claims] in reality is only a guise for more male dominance."[66]

---

65. Catherine MacKinnon, "Difference and Dominance," in MacKinnon, ed., *Feminism Unmodified* (Cambridge: Harvard University Press, 1987), p. 36.

66. Richard J. Ellis, *The Dark Side of the Left: Illiberal Egalitarianism in America* (Lawrence: University of Kansas Press, 1998).

Under such broad strokes it seems that not even the letters that make up the word *equality* can be viewed as exempt from the charge of male bias. It is no wonder that feminists are not even in the same playing field when it comes to finessing the intricacies of egalitarianism, let alone addressing the metaquestions about its rightness, justness, or proper balance with, for example, liberty.

Unfortunately, MacKinnon is not alone. Other feminist theorists have heeded her call and begun to add to the hysteria. Elizabeth Grosz has, on several occasions, reappropriated the term *equality* to mean something that is all about *difference*, warning women to stay away from traditional forms of egalitarianism:

> Try as it may, a feminism of equality is unable to theorize sexual and reproductive equality adequately. . . . In opposition to egalitarianism, a feminism based on the acknowledgment of women's specificities and oriented to the attainment of autonomy for women has emerged over the last ten years or more. . . . Only sameness or identity can ensure equality. In the case of feminists of difference, however, difference is not seen as difference *from* a pre-given norm, but as *pure difference*, difference in itself, difference with no identity. . . . For feminists, to claim women's difference from men is to reject existing definitions and categories, redefining oneself and the world according to women's own perspectives. . . . The right to equality entails the right to be the same as men; while struggles around the right to autonomy imply the right to either consider oneself equal to another or the right to reject the terms by which equality is measured and define oneself in different terms. It entails the right to be and to act differently.[67]

It seems that there just is no more room for misinterpretation. Feminist egalitarianism is not about egalitarianism at all.

So what do women want? They want to have all of the advantages of egalitarian justice—laws and rules that provide, at a mini-

67. Elizabeth Grosz, "Conclusion: A Note on Essentialism and Difference," in Sneja Gunew, ed., *Feminist Knowledge*, pp. 339–40.

mum, "equal freedom to pursue their goals without violence, equal possession of the necessities of life, equal opportunity to develop and utilize their talents to the fullest possible extent, equality of political and civil rights, and so forth"[68]—but they want all of this without a male definition of equality.

Unfortunately, according to such theorists, every "generalization," every "past ideology, literature, and philosophy is a product of male supremacy."[69] "Feminism highlights the hypocrisy and irrationality of these universalistic claims in the face of overt and tacit discriminatory practices."[70] In actuality, then, that the construct of even the concept of *equality* itself, let alone *violence, possession, necessity, opportunity, talent, politics,* or *rights* are, at the very least, not to be understood or debated in their usual way, let alone rationally embraced or rejected.

If we accept, however, with such radicals "that 'equality' on male terms is not enough," I genuinely query, again, what is it that women want?[71]

Women can be included as men's equals but only at the expense of recognizing a validation of women's specificity. Equality, then, involves a neut(e)ralization of the feminine. . . . Egalitarianism leaves the basic frameworks, methods, and assumptions of male theory unquestioned. . . . Even if it remains desirable for women to struggle towards equality with men, it is simply not possible to include

68. Alan Gewirth, "The Justification of Egalitarian Justice," in Flathman, ed., *Concepts in Social and Political Philosophy*, pp. 352, 366, 364.

69. One of the first citations of this kind can be found in Shulamith Firestone and Anne Koedt, "Redstockings Manifesto," in *Notes from the Second Year*, July 7, 1969, pp. 112–13. It is reprinted in Miriam Schneir, *Feminism in Our Time* (New York: Vintage, 1994), pp. 127–29.

70. Sandra Harding, *Whose Science? Whose Knowledge? Thinking from Women's Lives* (Ithaca: Cornell University Press, 1991), p. 32.

71. Robyn Rowland and Renate D. Klein, "Radical Feminism: Critique and Construct," in Sneja Gunew, ed., *Feminist Knowledge*, p. 274.

women in those theories (and daily tasks) from which they have been excluded.[72]

Why is it impossible? Because women's bodies are different from men's. Then, what has happened to the desire for equity?

It seems that we have come full circle. What started as an attempt by first-generation feminists to deny an essential bodily difference—in order to set themselves up as being equal to men, deserving of all the rights and privileges afforded to men, being thus essentially the same—has ended in the second-generation claim that what is most important to the egalitarian feminist is some kind of fundamental difference. Accordingly, even the most straightforward form of equality, formal equity, is reappropriated, redefined, and expanded to mean something highly problematic. "The principle of formal equality: Like cases should be treated alike; differences of treatment should reflect *genuine* and *relevant*, as opposed to mythic-stereotypical and irrelevant, differences between the sexes."[73] Of course, what counts as genuine and relevant is not developed, and there are feminist reasons why such development may not be forthcoming.

What counts, for example, as genuine may require one to make empirical claims about the genuine (i.e., biological?) difference between men and women. This would of course require some serious science, and science, so says feminism, is itself seriously infected.[74] Furthermore, is it not the biological assumption that is assumed to be the most mythical?

72. Grosz, "Philosophy," in Gunew, ed., *Feminist Knowledge*, pp. 158–59.

73. Elizabeth Rapaport, "Generalizing Gender: Reason and Essence in the Legal Thought of Catherine MacKinnon," in Louise M. Antony and Charlotte Witt, eds., *A Mind of One's Own*, p. 128, my emphasis.

74. For an account of this claim as well as a critical response see E. R. Klein, "Criticizing the Feminist Critique of Objectivty," *Reason Papers* 18 (Fall 1993), pp. 289–97.

And this is only the tip of the feminist apostasy iceberg. Many feminists claim that

> a large part of the responsibility for societal injustices lies deep within science itself. . . . If one's going to go deeper politically and criticize the presuppositions of liberal political theory, then one must coordinately go deeper conceptually and criticize the presuppositions of the epistemology and metaphysics that underwrite the politics.[75]

Such digging, however, shows only their own peculiar brand of myth-making and none of the essential biases feminists are so wont to expose.[76]

IMPLICATIONS FOR A FREE SOCIETY

> *Beware of all spirits that lie in chains! Of clever women, for example, whom fate has confined to a petty, dull environment, and who grow old there. It is true they lie apparently sluggish and half-blind in the sunlight; but at every unfamiliar step, at everything unexpected, they start up and bite; they take their revenge on everything that has escaped from their dog-kennel.*
>
> —Friedrich Nietzsche[77]

From first-generation political agendas, to their second-generation critiques of traditional science's commitment to objectivity as well as classical epistemology's commitment to reason,[78] in the final

---

75. Louise M. Antony, "Quine as Feminist: The Radical Import of Naturalized Epistemology," in Antony and Witt, eds., *A Mind of One's Own*, p. 204.

76. If one is interested in wading through the epistemological muck, see, for example, a counterargument to the position that science and/or epistemology is fundamentally sexist, in Klein, *Feminism under Fire*.

77. Friedrich Nietzsche, *Daybreak: Thoughts on the Predjudices of Morality*, ed. Maudemarie Clark and Brian Leiter (Cambridge: Cambridge University Press, 1997), p. 227.

78. For a critique of this move, see E. R. Klein, "Sorry Virginia, There Is No Feminist Science," in James P. Sterba, *Controversies in Feminism* (New York: Rowman and Littlefield, 2001), pp. 131–54.

analysis, all roads trodden by contemporary feminists lead to the same goal—the single-minded valuing of themselves *qua* women under the banner: The personal is political!

Under the wide petticoat provided by such a slogan, however, a great deal of tyranny can be hidden. Women can, with their political left hand, argue for an equality in the workplace that is consistent with traditionally liberal, albeit male, democratic principles. At the same time, with their other hand, they are free to argue for their peculiar and special status at home—due to their role as the primary caretaker of children. In other words, they want exactly what men want, except they also want more. "All women are subtle in exaggerating their weaknesses in order to appear as utterly fragile ornaments who are hurt even by a speck of dust. Their existence is supposed to make men feel clumsy, and guilty on that score. Thus they defend themselves against the strong and 'the law of the jungle.'"[79]

Although it is true that not all contemporary feminists are ready to admit to buying into the above theoretical commitment to equity as difference,[80] when they are ready to get personal, it seems that all feminists enjoy being treated more like ladies than like equals.

Feminists, like Goldilocks, may want equality but they do not want it to be too cold or too hot. Unfortunately, "just right" for

79. Nietzsche, *The Gay Science*, p. 66.

80. For example, Louise M. Antony, "'Human Nature' and Its Role in Feminist Theory," in Kourany, ed., *Philosophy in a Feminist Voice*, p. 67, claims that "feminist theory needs to appeal to a universal human nature in order to articulate and defend its critical claims about the damage done to women under patriarchy, and also to ground its positive vision of equitable and sustainable human relationships." And that "as long as women and men share certain morally relevant capacities—the capacity for rationally directed action, the capacity to form emotional attachments, the capacity to communicate—general norms of human flourishing will still apply equally to both," p. 86.

feminists will require them to at least spoil, if not simply consume, someone else's porridge.

For example, although many women were obviously interested in being treated equally under the law, such interest was quite selective. That is, when it came to the statutory rape laws argued in the courts in the 1980s, feminists never bothered to insist that the law (which made sex with a female underage partner illegal) be broadened to include sex with an underage male partner.[81] Instead they have spent the last two decades attempting to reconstruct the entire definition of rape to broaden it to include marital rape, date rape, and for some, every act of sex between a man and a woman.[82]

In addition, feminists seem to be blatantly inconsistent when it comes to the military. Although women clearly want to be able to take advantage of the benefits (e.g., loans, health care, and pensions) and privileges of military service, they do not seem to be insisting on equality when it comes to the mandatory draft that still exists. Given that the "cultural limits"[83] reached by such "male" institutions as the Supreme Court never deterred women from arguing for the equality of their own benefits, when it comes to consistency they leave much to be desired. It may be that "feminists have a duty to make sure that women have access to every echelon of military service,"[84] but there seems to be no correlative duty to ensure that women are part of a mandatory sign-up at eighteen. When the "inherently oppressive" institution known as the United State government has protected women from being drafted since the inception of the country and now, when performing equal

81. This law has recently been broadened to include statutory rape by women; however, such broadening did not come at the hands of feminists.
82. For the details of this argument see E. R. Klein, "Date Rape: The Feminist Construct That's Harmful to Women," *Contemporary Philosophy*, vol. 23, nos. 1 and 2 (2001).
83. Rappaport, "Generalizing Gender," in Antony and Witt, eds., *A Mind of One's Own*, p. 128.
84. Baumgardner and Richards, *Manifesta*, p. 280.

duties is really on the line—duties that, during a time of war, come with a serious risk—feminists and their arguments for egalitarianism are nowhere to be found. It seems that not all "male biases" are harmful and in need of restructuring.

And workplace legislation is similarly problematic. With respect to, for example, the Family and Medical Leave Act of 1993 (FMLA),[85] which grants "a family temporary medical leave under certain circumstances," ostensibly allows both women and men the chance to avoid workplace discrimination when caring for a new-born child, a handicapped family member or an elderly parent. Although the argument for protection was not clear, under the equal protection clause of the Fourteenth Amendment, the argument for the protection to be viewed as gender-neutral was.

Interesting, however, is that in one of the FMLA findings, Congress lists as "one of the reasons" it must support the Act is that "due to the nature of roles of men and women in our society, the primary responsibility for family caretaking often falls on women, and such responsibility affects the working lives of women more than it affects the working lives of men."[86] Therefore, the FMLA was put on the books not in a spirit of gender neutrality but, on the contrary, primarily in order to protect women. Despite the posturings by feminist egalitarians concerning anything based on gender distinctions, feminists are not found grumbling about what could easily be taken as sexist findings for, again in this case, the inequality worked to favor women.[87]

Is all of this inequality in the name of feminist egalitarianism simply an oversight by the overzealous? I do not think so. Susan Moller Okin, for example, argues quite vociferously for the "dem-

85. Public Law 103-3, enacted on February 5, 1993.
86. Family and Medical Leave Act of 1993, Findings 5.
87. It is suggested that such findings are merely a product of contemporary American culture. Whether this is true is outside the scope of this chapter.

olition, abolition and disappearance of gender,"[88] meaning, however, only that the state should forbid gendered practices "that make women and children vulnerable."[89] And Janet Radcliffe Richards states that:

> We want good doctors, certainly, but at the same time we want to encourage people to think of women as doctors. *If, as a matter of fact,* we think that the best way to achieve this is to have a good many successful women doctors, we may consider making rules which allow women to become a doctor with slightly lower medical qualifications than a man.[90]

The arguing for, or acceptance of, blatantly gendered practices such as the ones listed—which favor women at the expense of, at least men, if not important medical standards that affect us all—make this peculiar brand of inequality at least at odds with egalitarianism, if not fundamentally sexist.

One example of how feminists' desire for equality shows itself to be nothing but a power play concerns the use and abuse of Title IX legislation.[91] Feminist social activists have, in the name of equity, forced many college sports programs to fold.[92] Debates concerning

88. Susan Moller Okin, *Justice Gender and the Family* (New York: Basic Books, 1989), pp. 105, 116.

89. Okin, "Humanist Liberalism," in Nancy Rosenblum, ed., *Liberalism and the Moral Life* (Cambridge: Harvard University Press, 1989), p. 53; Okin, *Justice Gender and the Family*, p. 172.

90. Janet Radcliffe Richards, *The Skeptical Feminist* (San Francisco: Harper and Row, 1982), p. 143.

91. Title IX Education Amendments, 1972, ensure that there is gender equity in educational settings.

92. Interestingly, there have been some attempts to answer the empirical questions of who actually calls oneself a feminist today, and what, exactly, such persons claim to be doing to support their beliefs. See, e.g., Faye J. Crosby, Janet Todd, and Judith Worell, "Have Feminists Abandonded Social Activism? Voices from the Academy," in Leo Montada and Melvin J. Lerner, eds., *Current Societal Concerns about Justice* (New York: Plenum Press, 1996), pp. 85–102. More interesting are the kinds of self-justifying and petty concerns that count as activism, e.g., "participating on women's studies coordinating committees," p. 100–101.

the value of such teams aside, in order to comply with federal Title IX regulations concerning gender equity in college sports, when feminists have whined that despite the market factors—high cost, low turnout—women's sports deserve the same financial support as men's, everyone jumps. Because of the law, in order to comply and yet stay solvent, "colleges and universities are increasingly dropping men's athletic teams rather than support women's teams."[93]

And this is only one small example. Feminist egalitarians have argued that the state has a duty to provide women with

> equal access to health care, regardless of income, which includes coverage equivalent to men's, though keeping in mind that women use the system more often than men do because of our reproductive capacity . . . while safeguarding a woman's rights to bear (or not to bear) a child, regardless of circumstances, including women who are younger that eighteen or impoverished.[94]

Feminist egalitarians, then, are really arguing for equality plus more—more, that is, for women. And such theorists argue for equality plus more even though such laws would, at the very least, serve as yet one more excuse for "a bloated bureaucracy in all the state capitals and in Washington, D.C."[95]

More seriously, such laws, protecting the poor in general, but in particular poor women who believe they have a special right to have children at the state's expense—"produce children but take little care to ensure their economic security"[96]—not only create a larger number of poor, but encourage the development of a culture that has no respect for personal responsibility. Finally, and most

93. Peter Monaghan, "Dropping Men's Teams To Comply with Title IX," *The Chronicle of Higher Education*, December 4, 1998, pp. A41–A42.

94. Baumgardner and Richards, *Manifesta*, pp. 278–281.

95. Tibor Machan, "Utopian Americans and False Guilt about the Poor," in *Liberty and Culture*, p. 275.

96. Tibor Machan, "Demythologizing the Poor," in *Liberty and Culture*, p. 277.

important, such laws could, in the long term, run all of us out of money, jeopardizing the economy (and therefore the national security) of the United States.[97]

And, for some feminist egalitarians, too much is still not enough, because the poor who have been awarded every social benefit are nonetheless oppressed.

> Those who are in extreme need, although equal in worth to those who help them, are nonetheless not equal in circumstance or capacity, and in this sense they do not have equal standing necessary for justice to demand that they make a return . . . and they find this inequality painful and humiliating.[98]

Under these conditions it is no wonder that the social welfare system in the United States is unequal and sexist: Given that women, due to their reproductive capabilities, are more needy then men, and given that anyone who needs more may have to take more (combined with the foregoing claim that anyone who takes more will ultimately feel pain, and, of course, forcing women to feel pain and humiliation is fundamentally sexist), therefore, the welfare state in this country is fundamentally sexist.

Interestingly, however, so is the free market. The free market is oppressive according to feminist egalitarians because the marketplace is itself sexist for the "gendered division of labor has serious and direct impact on the opportunities of girls and women."[99]

---

97. See, e.g., Lawrence H. Starkey, "Ethical Judgments on Relations between Rich and Poor," *Contemporary Philosophy* 22, no. 1–2 (2000): 7–11. On a humorous note, I recall one of the skits from *Monty Python's Flying Circus* in which Robin Hood continues stealing from the now destitute "rich" to feed the new wealthy "poor."

98. Jean Hampton, "Feminist Contractarianism," in Antony and Witte, eds., *A Mind of One's Own*, p. 255, n. 54.

99. Okin, "Gender Inequality and Cultural Differences," *Political Theory* 22, no. 1 (February 1994): 12.

The right of the individual to the pursuit of liberty and progress is acted out, in liberal theory, against an assumed background of certain kinds of labouring and ownership relations. These relations are, implicitly and historically, relations between men. These relations between men are made possible by, and sustained by, the political and economic subjection of women. In other words, the free-enterprise "equality" between men necessarily excludes the participation of women *on an equal footing* . . . This notion of free-enterprise "equality" is an ideal that is based on the "freedom and equality" of men in market relations that in turn presupposes the unpaid labour of women. As such one can attempt to bring women "up to" the stage of labour market relations to ensure their equality with men without questioning the domestic basis of these relations but then this will have the consequence of either doubling women's workload or obscuring the political and economic functions of the domestic sphere. There is a third "option," which is for women to "become men," that is for women to function in the public sphere "as if" they are men. However, even this option disadvantages women, both individually and as a group. It disadvantages women individually in that they do not have the benefit, as do their competitors, of an unpaid domestic worker. It disadvantages women as a group in that if they do not reproduce they are not able to consolidate and accumulate wealth through inheritance.[100]

The sympathetic reading of the previous quote is that the market is already biased against women, that is, inherently unequal; therefore, any additional inequalities added to harm men can be seen only as balancing the scales toward real equality; in other words, two wrongs make a right.

Of course such objective, universal notions such as wrong and right, under feminists' interpretations, are nothing less than sexist constructs, and so the unsympathetic reading must be given. Feminist egalitarians cannot want equal rights, not only because their

100. Moira Gatens, *Feminism and Philosophy: Perspectives on Difference and Equality* (Bloomingon: Indiana University Press, 1991), p. 44–46.

peculiar brand of egalitarianism reappropriates the term *equal* to mean *different* but because their feminism insists on deconstructing any and all value.[101] Feminists of any stripe do not want anything like equal rights, they want power. And they want this power at any cost.

This can best be illustrated by looking at the claims made by those feminists who, unlike the theorists discussed previously, actually claim to be free-market feminists. Free-market feminists, however, are no more interested in negotiating a reasonable notion of a free market than the egalitarian feminists were interested in equality.

The free-market economy of, for example, the United States is built on the ideas of Adam Smith[102] concerning laissez-faire capitalism, known today as a market-capitalist economy.

> In a market-capitalist economy, the economic entities are either individuals or enterprises (firms, farms, and whatnot) that are privately owned by individuals and groups, and not, for the most part, by the state. The main goal of these entities is economic gain in the form of wages, profits, interest, and rent. . . . Innumerable independent but competing actors, each acting from rather narrow self-regarding interests and guided by the information supplied by markets, produces goods and services much more efficiently than known alternatives.[103]

Is this really what the free-market feminist is after?

Although the free-market feminist is against, for example, state-

---

101. Contemporary feminism does not realize the consequence of its having flippantly dubbed all objective principles "male." In so doing it has made a commitment to epistemological and ethical relativism de facto. As such, two values in conflict can only end by "fighting." See W. V. Quine, "On the Nature of Moral Values," *Theories and Things*, pp. 55–66.

102. Adam Smith, *The Wealth of Nations*.

103. Robert A. Dahl, *On Democracy* (New Haven: Yale University Press, 1998), p. 167.

provided or even subsidized health care, the reasons they are against such social programs is not for the usual anti-egalitarian or libertarian reasons such as those cited previously. Instead, the free-market feminists' "objection to state-provided or subsidized childcare is that it denies women the opportunity to be full-time mothers, or, at least, primary caretakers."[104] After all, women want to be able to stay home and they want their labor at home to be paid for as if it were being performed in the marketplace.

But such bravado is obviously much more feminist than free-market, because a true emphasis on free-market housework would lead to *The Man Show*[105] scenario of competition that I do not believe most feminists would like. Housework and childrearing would have to be looked at solely as forms of labor and production whose only goal is the accumulation of capital. Women would compete for the "job" of being someone's wife—housewife and/or mother—or, if she wished to remain single, of proving that the children she produced would somehow be worth some stranger's capital investment. Although this may, in the final analysis, produce better wives and mothers, I doubt it is what feminists have in mind when they flippantly claim that nonmarket activities such as housework and childcare should be added into the Gross Domestic Product figures to "lend some dignity to the position of housewives."[106]

104. David Conway, "Free-Market Feminism," in David Conway, ed., *Free-Market Feminism* (London: IEA Health and Welfare Unit, 1998), p. 42.

105. *The Man Show* on the Comedy Central network spoofs most of contemporary culture regarding the relationships between men and women. The episode I am referring to aired March 3, 2001. Another episode actually had women enroll in "wise college" where women learned to pour beer, be less yacky, and never complain about their periods.

106. Barbara Bergmann, *The Chronicle of Higher Education*, December 1, 1993, p. A9.

CONCLUSIONS

A few hours of mountain climbing turn a villain and a saint into two rather equal creatures. Exhaustion is the shortest way to equality and fraternity—and liberty is added eventually by sleep.
—Freierich Nietzsche[107]

"Nietzsche fears that our post-Christian, liberal and democratic emphasis on equality and rights is eroding the sociopolitical conditions for the flourishing of human greatness."[108] I urge, instead, that it is feminism.

In the final analysis, not only are the important questions—Are free-markets better than welfare states? Are egalitarian constructs, no matter how finessed, inconsistent with basic liberties?—left unanswered, but after dancing with the feminists, one feels as if ground has actually been lost.

It is sad but true that what began as a legitimate political movement to acquire equality under the law has turned into something that is barely worth spoofing, let alone taking seriously when determining social policy. What began as a movement to end sexism, sexist exploitation, and oppression has ended in ridiculous claims offered to rationalize women's antimale sentiments.[109]

I urge anyone interested in the questions discussed here not to take feminist theorizing on this subject seriously. Nonfeminist egalitarians are interested in, for example, which is the most just theory of distribution—attempting to make interesting distinctions be-

---

107. Nietzsche, "The Wanderer and His Shadow," *Human, All Too Human*, p. 263.

108. Ruth Abbey and Friedrich Appel, "Domesticating Nietzsche: A Response to Mark Warren," *Political Theory* 27, no.1 (February 1999): 124.

109. One progressive feminist, bell hooks [sic!], has made some moves to acknowledge this in *Feminism Is for Everybody: Passionate Politics* (Cambridge, Mass.: South End Press, 2000), pp. 1–3.

tween those traits that are merely a product of luck and those that are due to one's voluntary choices.[110] All the while feminist egalitarians are claiming that, with respect to women, no action is truly voluntary, and there is no such thing as justice (given that it has been traditionally defined by men) anyway.

Neither side of this debate should bother with such feminist theories. Those who are sympathetic to the political right, happily, are well within their rights simply to ignore the arguments proposed by feminists because there really is not anything of substance there to dispute. Conservative women have, I believe, realized that feminists are simply not interested in maintaining their treasured commitments to individual responsibility and liberty.

To those women from the left, however, it must be realized that feminist egalitarianism is more interested in *difference* than *equality*, more interested in supporting their own theoretical agenda than the needs of actual women. Given that feminist commitments to egalitarianism have little to do with any historical, philosophical, or economic notion of equity, they must tighten their liberal belts and recognize that with "sisters" like these, who needs enemies?

110. See, e.g., Richard J. Arneson, "Luck Egalitarianism and Prioritarianism," in *Ethics* 110, no. 3 (January 2001): 339–49.

CHAPTER FOUR

Equality and Liberty
as Complements

Mark LeBar

THE IDEALS OF EQUALITY and liberty are twin pillars of modern democratic attitudes. We believe they underwrite our commitments to our cherished political institutions and our relations among ourselves as citizens. Yet it is not so obvious that these pillars stand together. In a perfectly free world, some of us would no doubt fare well whereas others would not. Even if we begin with equal amounts of wealth, given the differences in our abilities and enterprise, the freedom to do what we wish with it will threaten that equality. And a world in which each of us was assured a roughly equal degree of material welfare would require massive constraints on our liberty. The broken promises of twentieth-century socialism suggest that if equality is used to justify political institutions, liberty is quickly extinguished.

Is it then right to see equality and liberty as in tension with each other? If we want to avoid that conclusion, we might begin by suspecting that we have got hold of the wrong conceptions of either liberty or equality, or both. Perhaps material equality is not the form of equality that is of greatest moral and political value. Perhaps, on the other hand, the freedom to do what you wish with what you have is not the most important notion of liberty. The right conceptions of both ideals might eliminate the tension between them. So I will suggest in this chapter.

But what conceptions are the right ones? In what follows I survey some of the candidates that philosophers and theorists have offered in the brief history of modern democracy. That history is littered with problematic conceptions of equality and liberty. I will suggest that the most promising approach (though one in need of much development itself) is one proposed by Immanuel Kant—a revered figure in moral philosophy, but unjustly overlooked as a source of political insight.

EQUALITY AS A VALUE

Equality figures greatly in our understanding of what is politically sacrosanct. The Declaration of Independence takes as a "self-evident" truth that "all men are created equal," and in doing so it lays claim to an ideal that we have tried valiantly to realize. But in what way are we equal? What kind of equality should matter for political institutions?

It patently cannot be equality of any sort of natural attribute. There is simply no denying that we differ from each other in more ways than we can count, but these differences do not affect our conviction that we are equal in some important sense. Equality must be a normative, not a descriptive, ideal; it must be a matter not of what we are like, but rather of how we ought to treat each other. The claim of the Declaration of Independence is that people should be treated as equals, not that people are equal in any biological sense.

But what does it mean to treat people as equals? How are political institutions capable of reflecting or embodying such an ideal? These are the questions that advocates of the ideal of material equality of various sorts—egalitarians—themselves disagree about.

Equality of Welfare

We might begin with the idea that treating people as equals means ensuring that, by and large, they live equally well, or have equally valuable or desirable lives. Some, indeed, have argued that political institutions ought to be arranged to ensure equality of welfare or equality of condition. We can appreciate the motivation for this idea by recognizing the role of brute luck in how desirable our lives are. My life is a much better one, given the time and circumstances of my birth and the parents to whom I was born, than it would have been had I been born a century before, or born into severe poverty. In one important sense it is just my luck that I was not. And there is something attractive about the idea that one job for human beings in community—in particular as part of their political organization—should be to minimize these unfair results of nature's crapshoot. As John Rawls, a prominent proponent of one form of egalitarianism, puts the point, a just society is one in which "men agree to share one another's fate"[1] by attempting to counteract the arbitrary natural distribution of advantages and disadvantages in our institutions. And one way to do this is to distribute the goods we produce so as to equalize the conditions in which we live our lives. The aim is to ensure that all of us live roughly equally well.

Plausible as this proposal sounds initially, it confronts two significant problems. First, such a proposal must include an account of how such welfare or well-being is to be measured, if we are to equalize it. This is a sizable problem. Is there some objective list of things we can check off and sum up for each person to arrive at a measurement of how well each is living? What would go on such a list, and who decides that? Consider a good as fungible as financial wealth. If we were to equalize the wealth of Bill Gates and the

---

1. John Rawls, *A Theory of Justice* (Cambridge: Harvard University Press, 1971).

Dalai Lama, would that make them equally well off? By whose standards? It seems doubtful that financial wealth matters to each of them in the same way. In general, it is hard to imagine any objective list of things to measure the desirability of lives that would command consensus. Though there are certainly broad areas of convergence (most of us would rather have more money than less), there is also great difference among the standards we use to judge how well our lives are going.

One way of avoiding that problem is this: instead of equalizing people's holdings in some fixed list of good things (which people may or may not value, or value to differing degrees), focus instead on equalizing the degree to which they have what they do value— the degree to which their own preferences are satisfied. Given this interpretation of equality of welfare, it does not matter that Bill Gates and the Dalai Lama do not have the same amount of money. What matters is that each has what he wants to a roughly equal degree, though what that is for each is very different.

But this approach too has its drawbacks. What if what I want is prohibitively costly? What if I can be happy only if I have uninterrupted opportunity to gaze on original Renoirs and will be deeply unhappy otherwise? Does a commitment to equality require that I be ensured uninterrupted access to the paintings? What if my preference is something less bizarre but more perverse, such as the reinstitution of slavery? Is there the slightest reason for our political system to be designed so that I get equal satisfaction of that preference? Presumably not. Clearly not just any preference I have should count for purposes of measuring my well-being, and thus for equalizing my well-being with that of my fellow citizens.

Moreover, my claims to the satisfaction of my preferences are even weaker if I have deliberately cultivated those preferences. If they are my doing (so to speak), the fact that I could have cultivated other, less costly or less perverse, preferences further undermines my claim on society for their satisfaction. This brings us to the second serious problem for equality of welfare of which I spoke earlier, and egalitarians differ deeply as to how to deal with it. Whether and how our responsibility for our preferences matters is a specific case of a more general worry: how are we to reconcile equality of welfare with the idea that each of us must be thought to bear (some) responsibility for how well our lives go? We are not just victims of fate with respect to our well-being. We are agents who act to make our lives better or worse, and we hold each other accountable for much of how well we live. These facts matter for our thinking about equality.

For example, suppose we think that society ought to be ordered so that each person fares equally well (by some metric or other) in their lives, and we distribute goods accordingly. But someone, call him Burt, loves to gamble. Unfortunately (for Burt) he is not good at it, and consequently he loses money as fast as he can get his hands on it. If we attempt to give him more money for food, clothing, housing, and so on to bring his welfare up to a level of equality with others, he will just lose it gambling. Does a commitment to equality require that we keep funneling money to Burt in an effort to maintain his level of welfare at par with the welfare of others?

Equality of Resources

Proponents of egalitarianism deal in different ways with the idea that we bear some responsibility for our own well-being. One way is to insist that, instead of aiming for equality of welfare as an outcome, political institutions should provide for equality of resources, leaving individuals to bear the responsibility for how they deploy those resources and consequently for what level of well-being they achieve.[2]

2. Ronald Dworkin is among the most prominent proponents of this ap-

According to this approach, each of us is to have something like an endowment we value equally to the endowment of each other person. It will be up to each of us how we dispose of the resources with which we are endowed. We can invest them wisely and build on them, dispose of them foolishly (perhaps gamble them away), or something in between. The point is that in this conception of the ideal of equality, we are equal in terms of our entitlement to resources with which to live our lives. Society owes us no more. If we squander our entitlement, there is no obligation in terms of equality for society to restore what we have lost.

This way of thinking about the value of equality has the virtue of accommodating our intuitions about our responsibility for our own lives. Yet it does not square properly with other intuitions, even those held by other egalitarians. One complaint is this: if we are really concerned about leveling out the effects of the "natural lottery" that bear on our prospects for living desirable lives, equalizing resources fails to come to grips with a major way nature determines those prospects, in not attending to our individual capacities to utilize the resources we have. For example, a blind person, or a mentally impaired person, will simply not be able to accomplish as much with some resources as will persons with normal sight and normal cognitive capacities. What matters, for critics of resource egalitarianism, is not what resources we have, but what we are able to do with those resources.

There is a natural way for the resource egalitarian to respond to this objection, of course, and that is to insist that we ought to count such handicaps or limitations (or, better, the absence of them) as part of the total package of resources with which each of us is endowed—and which is to be equalized to the endowments of others. But this response is itself problematic. For one thing, the

proach. Ronald Dworkin, *Sovereign Virtue* (Cambridge: Harvard University Press, 2000).

notion of resources now reaches beyond what we have, to include what we are. Moreover, how are we to assess how much such limitations (or the lack of them) should count as part of our endowments? We can make reasonable accommodations for some handicaps, but for others we cannot. Even for those we can to some degree accommodate, this only mitigates inequalities, rather than equalizing the resources each of us has. How much more land, money, or other resource should go to a blind person to compensate for his or her handicap?

The resource egalitarian may instead bite the bullet and insist that each of us is responsible, not only for making the best of the share of resources we receive, but also for shaping our preferences in response to what our capabilities allow. My natural abilities (or lack of them) may prohibit me from ever playing third base in the major leagues, but the right thing is not for society to compensate me for that limitation, but for me to learn to work around it, to develop different ambitions more in keeping with what I can do. Persons with more severe handicaps, likewise, need to do the same. Blindness may prevent one from being an airline pilot, but it is not society's responsibility to compensate for that. Blind people, like everybody else, are responsible for finding ways to live well with a share of resources equal to the shares of everyone else.

Equality of Opportunity

At this point, critics of resource egalitarianism insist that the approach has lost touch with the intuitions that motivate egalitarianism in the first place. Not all our preferences are plausibly chalked up to choices we make and may rightly be held responsible for. Cases of severe impairment prevent the satisfaction of needs and desires that are common to any plausible conception of a good human life. The sensible thing to do is to recognize that, in focusing on resources themselves, this form of egalitarianism has somehow missed the point. What we care about is, roughly, having equal chances at living well. Although we are responsible for that to some degree, the best way to capture what we want to equalize is our opportunity for living well. Our opportunities are determined not only by what we have but also by what we are capable of doing with what we have. Those opportunities are the appropriate focus of egalitarian concern, and they are what our political institutions should attempt to equalize.[3]

Yet this approach brings with it its own problems. It needs ways of measuring not only welfare but also opportunity. If you and I both have the opportunity to become bankers, but you also have the opportunity to be a grocer, arguably you have greater opportunity than I. But what if, instead of being a grocer as an alternative, I could be a cashier or a schoolteacher? How do we go about measuring the opportunities people have, except in the rough way we judge that a well-educated child of a wealthy and well-connected family has more opportunity than a poorly educated child living in poverty? Is it possible to arrive at anywhere near enough precision in comparing the opportunities people have, to be able to fix on what an equal amount of opportunity would be?

A further problem is that once we begin assessing lists of options as a measure of opportunity, we have introduced the idea that it is not only welfare, or even the opportunity of improving on it, that we care about, but the liberty to determine for ourselves how we shall proceed from among a number of options. This way of thinking about the value of equality threatens to convert it into a way of thinking about the value of liberty.

Moreover, the idea that we deserve equal opportunity for welfare forces us to confront once again the problem of specifying

3. Richard Arneson has been a noted proponent of this form of egalitarianism. Richard Arneson, "Freedom and Desire," *Canadian Journal of Philosophy* 15 (1985): 425–48.

exactly what is going to count as welfare. This was a problem averted, to some degree, by the focus on resources, but here it returns in full flower. If both you and I could become bankers, but you would detest such a career whereas I would like nothing better, do we have equal opportunity for welfare? Apparently not. But what if nothing would give you the satisfaction I can get from banking except being a world-champion ice skater? How can we equalize our opportunities for welfare under such conditions?

The problem, once again, is that we ourselves have a great deal of say in how well our lives go, and in how much satisfaction we can get from them, and many egalitarians are not comfortable with the thought that society ought to be hostage to the way we dispose of our responsibilities for our own well-being. What is wanted is a conception of what should be equalized that is objective enough to resist the vagaries of perverse or expensive preferences and desires, but which has enough flexibility to reflect the fact that differences in individual abilities to take advantage of resources are important determinants of how well people live. Is there such a thing? Egalitarians certainly aspire to specify it. But even if they do, there is another important element of the picture that has not yet been accounted for: we have paid insufficient attention (in fact no attention at all) to where those resources come from.

The Production Problem

How can a fundamental commitment to equality as a political value allow for the fact that it takes people and effort to produce the goods that go into our calculations about equal distribution? Some egalitarians offer answers to this question, but they are less than satisfactory.

One gambit is to refuse the question. The egalitarian might insist that equality is an ideal to be applied at whatever level of goods may be available in a given society, at a given time. If the commitment to equality results in fewer goods being available to be divided—and thus a lower level of welfare than could be realized by at least some people if inequalities were allowed—then so much the worse for welfare. Equality is so important that it justifies bringing everyone down from the level of well-being they could enjoy if inequalities were tolerated.

But this is to bite a bullet that many egalitarians do not want to bite. A more plausible reply is to insist that what needs to be divided equally are not merely the benefits that social cooperation affords but also the burdens of effort and work necessary to realize those benefits. It would be a mistake to focus merely on the goods enjoyed by citizens as a result of productive activity; that activity itself needs to be counted as part of our endowments. We need, that is, to balance the benefits each of us has against the burdens it takes us to produce them, and to ensure that for each of us that balance comes out roughly the same.

This proposal introduces new difficulties. Some are simply complexities. Should labor count as a benefit or a burden? Some labor is obviously burdensome, at least to some people, whereas other labor is pleasurable, at least to some people. Perhaps most forms of labor have moments of both. Is there any hope for an adequate objective measure of the degree of benefit or burden a given form of work involves? If not, perhaps a focus on subjective preferences and reactions to labor is necessary. But once again, the introduction of public accommodation of subjective preferences brings concerns about perverse or expensive preferences—as to the burdens of labor just as with the benefits of goods.

But in any event the unpleasantness of labor is only remotely connected with the production of the goods and services that contribute to the benefits egalitarians want to distribute equally among us. If it matters to us that our society produces adequate wealth for all to live well, questions about how much suffering is involved in producing that wealth, or how that suffering is distributed, cannot be our only concern. What we also must care about is that people's energies are directed in ways that are productive of those goods and services, and this is what the proposal to equalize benefits and burdens does not address.

Egalitarians whose focus is material wealth and its distribution may insist at this point that they are not promoting such equality as the exclusive political value, that they expect it to be balanced in the design and aim of political institutions with the pursuit of other values, including liberty and perhaps the sheer production of wealth in goods of all kinds, to be distributed according to egalitarian norms. So, they might argue, it is not a problem that the value of equality itself does not take into account problems of sponsoring and promoting production; that problem is to be attended to as part of a comprehensive political theory, not as part of a narrow concern with understanding the value of equality as a political ideal.

But this response will not fly. Goods and services are produced by deploying resources (land, raw natural materials, etc.), which become goods through their deployment. Resource egalitarians are straightforwardly confronted with a tension between the values of wealth creation and equality of resources because these represent competing alternatives as to how resources should be allocated. Should political and legal institutions be shaped so that resources are directed to the uses most productive of the goods that contribute to good human lives? Or should they be allocated so that no person can legitimately envy the resources allocated to another person? There is no obvious reason to think these ways of dividing resources would coincide, and if they do not, the defender of resource egalitarianism must confront the question of whether equality is valuable enough as a political ideal to justify the loss in production of goods that equality of resources would engender.

The problem is only a bit less acute for welfare or opportunity egalitarians. There is no real difference between goods that are deployed to make lives go well (consumer goods) and goods used to produce those goods (capital goods). Both kinds of goods draw on resources and labor for their production; more consumer goods can be produced only at the cost of producing fewer capital goods (and, thus, eventually fewer consumer goods in the future). Principles of distribution for the goods that contribute to welfare, or the opportunity for it, thus inevitably limit the productive possibilities of those goods, and once again there is no obvious reason to suppose that a division of goods to equalize welfare or opportunity for it (assuming we could figure out what that would be) will even approximate a division of goods that builds wealth. One does not have to be committed to the idea that building wealth should be the exclusive or even primary goal of political institutions to worry about this. Wealth is what allows us to live lives most of us find better than the lives of people a millennium or even a century ago, and it is the accumulation of wealth that proponents of equality of welfare, resources, or opportunity are concerned to divide. Any egalitarian whose primary concern is the material condition of our lives must confront the degree to which his or her preferred conception of equality is worth the sacrifice of well-being, not only of those who are best off but also of those who are not.[4]

Of course, committed proponents of material equality may be willing to bite even this bullet. In any event, our rehearsal of conceptions of equality has not shown that equality as a political ideal is useless or a mistake, only that our intuitions about the value of equality are heterogeneous and perhaps confused. Certainly there is reason to wonder whether equal treatment of our fellows is best thought of as bringing about equal conditions, whether of welfare, resources, or opportunity. Any such proposal runs into complications arising from the fact that we are to a large degree responsible for the conditions we make for ourselves, that we have different

---

4. This is an issue John Rawls explicitly seeks to address in his second principle of justice. See Rawls, *A Theory of Justice*.

attitudes about what will make our lives go well, and that we cannot focus only on what we get but must also attend to how goods will be produced as well. This does not mean equality is an empty ideal, but it does suggest we might profit by looking elsewhere in trying to understand it. We will return to this suggestion after considering to what degree, if any, liberty as a political value is in any better shape.

LIBERTY AS A VALUE

Why do we care about liberty? The question may not seem that difficult, but the answer may help us understand what kind of liberty matters. We want to be able to decide for ourselves what we will do. The choices we make shape our lives, and nobody ought to be able to determine how our lives will go but us ourselves. Threats to liberty are constraints on the things we can viably choose to do, and it matters vitally to us that those choices are left up to us.

Negative Liberty

This is the way some defenders of the value of liberty (e.g., John Stuart Mill[5]) have understood it. We might think that what matters is that our range of choices be as unconstrained as possible. On this negative conception of liberty, our legal and political institutions ought to be designed to protect our basic rights against harm and interference and within those parameters allow each of us to choose to live how we will. We are more free when our fellows leave us more options, less free when they leave us fewer.[6]

As good as it sounds, this conception of liberty quickly gives rise

5. See J. S. Mill, *On Liberty* (1859; Reprint, Indianapolis: Hackett Publishing Co., 1978).

6. Isaiah Berlin, *Four Essays on Liberty* (Oxford: Oxford University Press, 1969).

to problems that redirect our attention away from the issue of limiting the interference of others.

The first problem is that if liberty is valuable because it is good to have lots of options from which to choose, maybe political institutions should focus on providing lots of options for people, rather than protecting their liberty. The poor, the sick, the incapacitated, do not enjoy the range of options the wealthy and healthy do. If having options is what matters, arguably providing them to those who have the fewest options is more important than protecting the options of those of us who already have our share and more.

Positive Liberty

This line of thought leads to a positive conception of freedom: the ability to set one's own goals and achieve them. I am positively free to the extent it is within my power to make of myself and my life what I will. The challenge of positive liberty is especially acute if we believe, as many do, that we should have equal liberty. Most of us think it is not right for some people to be guaranteed, as a matter of law and policy, more liberty than others. Freedom, like justice, loses something, if not everything, if one person has it only by depriving another of it. But if this intuition is right, then interpreting freedom as the possibility of choice among options takes a strongly egalitarian twist. Equalizing freedom then means equalizing the options that people have to choose from. We have turned from equality to liberty, only to make liberty over into equality.

A related problem awaits us if we think that liberty is important because it is instrumental to our capacity to achieve our goals. We might be tempted to think that liberty matters because we need it to get the other things worth having. But this way of thinking about the value of liberty quickly leads us down the same problematic path. If others interfere with us, that may indeed prevent us from achieving what we deem worth achieving. But the interference of others is hardly the only thing that may prevent us from doing so. Nature deprived me of the possibility of being a major-league third baseman or a concert pianist. Sheer poverty deprives people of the resources to undertake what they would most like to undertake. Lots of things may prevent us from achieving our aims, so it seems a mistake to focus on liberty as the essential element in being able to aspire to what we will.

What Is Missing

But this way of thinking about the value of liberty misses something important. There is a moral difference between my being unable to be a big-league ballplayer because I do not have the skills, and being unable to do so because, even though I have the skills, someone threatens my life if I try to play. Although it is too bad if I lack skills, that is not a moral issue; if someone forces me not to play, that surely is. Liberty does matter because of what we can do when we are free, but it may matter more because of what it signifies about how people are treating each other. The Kantian outlook I will propose takes very seriously this line of thought, and we will return to it later.

There is yet another problem with understanding liberty as having options from which to choose. How should we measure liberty so construed? We face a problem similar to the problem faced by the opportunity egalitarian. Suppose we consider two persons— one as free as any of us normally are, except that his thumbs are bound up in splints. The other is imprisoned, bound head and foot, and left with only the freedom of movement of her thumbs. But she still has indefinitely many options as to what to do with her thumbs, just as the first person still has indefinitely many options. We want to say that the first person is freer than the second, but is this due to the number of options he has open? How could we go about counting the number of options each has open? And would our count really be getting at our reasons for thinking the first has more freedom than the second? Does not something like the value of the options open to the respective persons matter in our thoughts about how much liberty they have?

Of course, we are now headed right back to the territory we just left—thinking not about what options are opened or closed, but about what value there is to the options we have. Something important about the moral point of freedom has been lost in the shuffle. Moreover, this way of thinking about liberty justifies gross intrusions on our commonsense conception of liberty. Suppose I kidnap you, imprison you, immobilize you, and force you to submit to a brainwashing regimen that consists of electric shocks and drugs. The effect of this regimen, however, is that all you can think about is a cure for cancer. I have so focused your brain activity that not only can you think of nothing else, but you do not want to. You want more than ever to think about this noble goal; it matters to you more than anything else. And you are free to do so. Does that mean I have not deprived you of freedom? The value of your sole remaining option is great on any account, even your own. But the fact that your only option is valuable does not seem to mean you are any the less unfree as a result of my actions.

I am not suggesting that there are not ways of tinkering with these conceptions of freedom to reduce their problematic consequences. But it is not clear that tinkering will yield a clear and compelling conception of freedom in the long run. The problems with our ordinary conceptions of freedom have led some thinkers to the conclusion that freedom is a useless concept for political theorizing. We do not have one concept, we have several, and they stand in uneasy tension with each other, incapable of being harmonized.[7]

---

7. This is Arneson's conclusion in "Freedom and Desire," *Canadian Journal*

But this conclusion is as premature as the comparable conclusion about equality. Presumably we want to reduce or eliminate the tension between the ideals if we hold out hope for political institutions that do not sacrifice one cherished ideal for the sake of another. What is true is that if we want a conception of equality that is compatible with the value we place on liberty, we actually have two problems, rather than one. But we appear to be as much at sea as to how to think about liberty as a political value as we were about equality. Perhaps the problems need to be solved together. That is the promise of the approach to which we now turn.

KANTIAN EQUALITY

We have seen that it is difficult to formulate precisely our ideals of liberty and equality. Not only may liberty and equality be in tension with each other, but also there seem to be internal tensions to our thinking about each of them as values.

One way of trying to resolve the tension has been to understand equality as formal equality. Roughly put, formal equality requires that equals be treated as equals, and unequals be treated as unequals. This is a simple and powerful form of justice; it is hard to argue with it, but for just that reason it does not get us very far. It leaves unspecified what are the pertinent ways in which we are equal or unequal, and what is to count as being treated as equally or unequally. Formal equality is as compatible with any of the forms of egalitarianism we have considered as it is with libertarian approaches that reject them.

Some have suggested that, for political purposes, formal equality is a demand for the rule of law—the idea that each person is to be

---

of Philosophy 15 (1985): 425–48. I borrow the comparison of the people with bound and free thumbs from him.

equally accountable to standards of legal justice.[8] But here too guidance is limited. Is a law that prohibits civil suits against a sitting president consistent with the rule of law? Any system of law distinguishes between persons in virtue of their office, if nothing else. How are we to know which distinctions are legitimate and which not? The problem is not that the idea is bad, it is that we need more direction to understand what it might mean for political institutions.

I suggest a different way of understanding both liberty and equality, a way that not only resolves their tension with each other but also fixes on an aspect of each ideal that seems to be at its heart. I will refer to this conception as *Kantian equality* for sake of simplicity, but it specifies a form of liberty as a political ideal just as it specifies a form of equality.

The view is found in the political writings of the great eighteenth-century German philosopher Immanuel Kant. Kant is best known for his ideas on the nature of the world and how we know it, and for his moral theory, which we will consider in a moment. But he also was a provocative political theorist, and at the foundation of his political philosophy is what he refers to as the Principle of Right:

> Any action is right if it can coexist with everyone's freedom in accordance with a universal law, or if on its maxim the freedom of choice of each can coexist with everyone's freedom in accordance with a universal law.[9]

Kant understands freedom, in the politically relevant sense, as "in-

8. This is Friedrich Hayek's suggestion. He says, "Equality of the general rules of law and conduct . . . is the only kind of equality conducive to liberty and the only equality which we can secure without destroying liberty." See Friedrich Hayek, *The Constitution of Liberty* (Chicago: University of Chicago Press, 1960), p. 85.

9. Immanuel Kant, *The Metaphysics of Morals*, trans. Gregor (Cambridge: Cambridge University Press, 1797/1991), p. 56.

dependence from being constrained by another's choice," and says our "innate right to freedom" includes *innate equality*, which is "independence from being bound by others to more than one can in turn bind them."[10] In other words, Kant believes that his idea of freedom entails or includes an important form of equality, and his idea of the form of equality that is politically relevant includes an important form of liberty. How can we understand these two ideas in a way that makes this so?

The Moral Foundation

The key to understanding Kant's view is grasping an idea that is at the heart of his moral theory. Kant's fundamental moral concern is with human beings as moral agents, as creatures that have the capacity to exercise will in choosing what to do. Of the first importance to Kant is how we do so, as reflected in the principles we elect to act upon. When it comes to our relations with others, Kant believes that we must also recognize others as having these same capacities, and respect them accordingly. We must see others' capacity for rational willing as giving them dignity, and as removing them from the realm of objects we may use as instruments in advancing our own projects and achieving our own goals. We must, as Kant puts it, see them as ends in themselves, never merely as means for us to dispose of as we will.

The focus in Kant's moral theory is thus on the relations we have with each other as willing beings. It does not, as in some theories, focus on human beings as subjects of pleasure or pain, happiness or unhappiness. What matters is not trying to advance the greater good. What matters is that we understand our capacity to choose what we will do and how we will live, and that we recognize and respect that capacity in others.

10. Ibid., p. 63.

This recognition underlies the Principle of Right in Kant's political theory. Political institutions are to be established so as to protect each person's willing capacities from the depredations and control of others. The principle of freedom Kant defends is one that attends not to the choices we have—to their number or scope—but to the interference of others with the range of choices we have. He is less concerned that we have such choices than that others do not arbitrarily deprive us of them. In this sense, the Kantian conception of freedom is like the negative conception we considered earlier. In fact, it constitutes a negative conception of freedom, but the rationale for it is not that it matters that we have choices, but instead that our choices not be limited or forced by others in arbitrary ways.

But of course anytime we act, we restrict the choices of others. If I buy the last maple bar at the doughnut shop, nobody else has the option of eating it. So do I violate their freedom in Kant's sense by taking it? There are at least two ways of trying to address this problem.

One is Kant's. In his moral theory Kant maintains that "good willing" is willing according to principles that could be universal law. If I consider taking the last maple bar as the practical expression of a principle that any rational being could accept, I see that even if I preclude you from taking it, I do not violate your freedom. After all, if the last maple bar is to be eaten at all, somebody has to eat it, and when they do, nobody else can do so. So the moral issue turns on the basis on which the somebody who gets that last maple bar is determined. And provided the system by which I am justified in taking it is rationally warranted (perhaps it is just a matter of being the next customer willing to pay for it) in Kant's sense my doing so violates nobody's freedom.

A different way of thinking about the problem is to consider my object or aim when I take the maple bar. Intuitively, there is a big difference between the objective of getting something tasty to eat and the objective of depriving someone else of something tasty to eat by taking it first. This way of thinking about the issue dovetails with Kant's proposal for thinking about willing. What we will is a function not just of the things we choose to do, but of our reasons for choosing to do them. If I deliberately aspire to frustrate your will, that manifests a lack of the kind of respect for you as a willing agent that Kant thinks is morally required of me. Certainly a principle that permitted deliberately frustrating the wills of others, merely for the sake of frustrating them, would not be a principle rational agents with wills of their own could accept. They could not rationally will both that they act purposively and that their wills are frustrated deliberately.

Political Implications

Kant's view of political institutions is that they should be designed to afford us the maximum degree of freedom from the latter sort of constraint, that is, having our own wills subordinated to the wills of others arbitrarily.[11] This idea emerges clearly in his conception of the politically relevant form of equality. Consider once again how Kant formulates that conception: "independence from being bound by others to more than one can in turn bind them." The suggestion here is that in cases of control by one person over another, there is an inequality in the degree to which the parties are subject to the other's will. One is subject to the other to a degree greater than the second is subject to the first. What is wrong in this condition is the inequality in the control of one person over an-

11. The requirement for maximum equal freedom is important. We could equalize freedom by allowing no freedom from the constraints of the wills of others. Kant is clear not only that equality is required but also that the equal freedom of each person from the constraints of the wills of others is to be as great as possible.

other. This is the notion of equality Kant thinks matters for political institutions.

In what sense might there be equal control between parties? To capture this idea, Kant borrows from Rousseau the concept of a general will. Although the details of this concept are complex, for our purposes its point is straightforward enough. The general will is, roughly, the united expression of will of every person who is subject to that will. The general will is an expression of all and only those things that each person subject to it can rationally accept. This means the general will is both a constraint on political institutions and is itself constrained by the wills of the governed.

This double-edged constraint works by imposing a test on legislation: to be permissible a law must command the endorsement of each member of society. Unless a proposed legal measure is rationally acceptable to each and every citizen, it may not acquire the force of law. This provides a protection against depredations in the name of the common good. Under Kant's concept of political Right, the common good is that which is acceptable to everyone subject to the laws. Citizens have rights against having their interests sacrificed for the interests of others.[12] Nor are the pet projects— even the projects with commendable motives and ends—of particular citizens entitled to support or endorsement from legal or political institutions. The particular commitments citizens may have do not provide reasons for legal constraints. Instead, the job of legal institutions is to secure freedom for citizens to pursue and honor their commitments as best they can without forcibly subordinating the wills of others to their own. The general will is constrained in that it can reflect only an equality of control of one citizen over another.

12. Here I depart a bit from the way Kant himself interprets the implications of these principles. For whatever reason, Kant believed they were consistent with a constitutional monarchy and strove to reduce any explicit conflict between his political principles and the government of Frederick the Great.

(Notice that this conception of the relation between freedom and equality has the virtue of explaining what is important about formal equality and the rule of law. We worry about violations of either because, when they occur, one person is arbitrarily exempted from the legal constraints by which others are bound.)

We might wonder whether the machinery of government can work under such constraints. If there are legal institutions at all, some people are going to be able to bind others more than they are subject to being bound by them. A judge, for example, exerts a degree of control over a convict's life to a far greater degree than the convict has control over the judge's life. How is this kind of inequality compatible with Kant's notion of innate equality?

One response would be to rely on a sort of hypothetical rational agreement. The idea would be that the criminal being judged is there by an act of his or her own will, so to speak, given that he or she must rationally will that crimes (of the sort he or she committed) be punished. This approach would obviously raise the bar as to what could count as a crime deserving of punishment. Because the specification of crimes is a function of the general will, only acts that command universal disapprobation could be criminalized; a single rational dissent is thus all that is required to disqualify something from being a crime. Perhaps this demanding standard for what can count as crime would be a good thing.[13] But the appeal to a sort of hypothetical rational agreement here ought to give us pause. As the story runs, what matters is not what the criminal does agree to, but what he or she should agree to given certain rational constraints on his or her judgment. But opinions as to what the criminal should agree to are a dime a dozen. Should we ground law on such an unstable basis?

---

13. Defenders of jury nullification argue that having juries judge the law as well as the facts in practice means that only one of twelve jurors in a criminal case need find the law unjustified or unjust in order to acquit, so that conviction would be possible only for crimes against which there is virtually unanimous sentiment.

A better approach, I think, is to grant that such exercises of unequal control are problematic for the very reason Kant says they are and thus are justifiable only if they are essential for the bare survival of the political society. Again, this is an extremely demanding condition. There are only a few governmental functions for which such a case can be made genuinely. But Kant's principle of right is a demanding principle. It puts genuine bite into the demand for liberty, understood as freedom from unequal degrees of constraint by others.

Even if these problems can be solved, further serious challenges for this proposal remain. First, if the principle demands being bound by others only to the degree that we can bind them, we need some way of measuring the degree to which one person binds (or can bind) another. If we have no way of measuring this, of course we have no way of equalizing the degree to which each person is bound. We ran into similar problems earlier when we considered opportunity egalitarianism and conceptions of freedom that focus on options. We should learn from those cases not to try to measure degree of control in terms of the number of options or choices that are given or taken from one person by another. But it is far from obvious what alternative avenues for characterizing equality of constraint might be more successful.

That is a problem in understanding precisely what the theory proposes, and how it should inform the structure of our legal and political institutions. But even if we were to get that cleared up, a further question remains, one that for many might represent an even more serious obstacle to accepting this as a theory of equality. Does it really capture what we think is important about our impulses toward equality? Is Kantian equality really the most important form of equality?

Answering "Yes" to this question means agreeing with Kant that what matters morally in our political institutions is fundamentally not how things turn out—in terms of how many people, or which people, lead desirable lives. What matters is how those institutions require or allow us to deal with other people as moral agents. Kant's radical proposal is that what matters is not the outcomes of our treatment of others, but the principles on which we act, and those principles must above all see others as rational beings whose choices we must respect.

Modern egalitarians will respond that either the proposal cannot be made sense of, or that once we do make sense of it, we see that it requires one of the forms of egalitarianism we have already found problematic, because this is what respecting the rational natures of others comes to. Some egalitarians (e.g., John Rawls) make this claim explicitly.

Careful argument will be required to meet this challenge, if it can be met, but Kantian equality offers the prospect of thinking in a different way about equality as a political value: not as a matter of distributing the goods we have, but as a moral relation among citizens that goes beyond the rule of law in explaining what matters in our treatment of each other. Kantian equality has not been the subject of much careful scrutiny, either by proponents of equality or by its critics; a distinctive and thorough development of this approach is yet to be seen. Given the problems with the alternatives, and given the Kantian clarion call for focus on respect for others, the problems of specifying what equal control between people really comes to and of defending the moral significance of this form of equality merit dedicated attempts at response. Kant's proposal is a way of thinking about both equality and liberty that bears further investigation.

INDEX

doctrine of natural rights, Hobbes and, 10; Locke and, 10–11; origin of, 10

"Domesticating Nietzsche: A Response to Mark Warren," *Political Theory* 27 (Abbey and Appel), 95*n*108

"Dropping Men's Teams to Comply with Title IX," *Chronicle of Higher Education* (Monaghan), 90*n*93

Dutch Revolution, 8

Dworkin, Ronald, xii, xiii, xiv, xv, xxiii, 69*n*25, 75, 101*n*2; egalitarian theory of, xiv; proposed use of government and, xiv; rights-based egalitarianism of, 79; types of rights and, 79

economic equality, 24; loss of economic benefits under, 25–26; political equality and, 23

egalitarian justice, feminist notion of, 82–83

egalitarianism, xi, 57, 99, 105, 107; absolute equality and, 63; beauty and, 59; Christian equality and, 7; classifications of, 73; conservatives and, xiii; definition of, 62; Dworkin, Ronald approach to, xiii–xv; economic effects of, xx; elitist notions of, xxi; feminism and, 64*n*11, 84; forms of, 65*n*12; ideal of, xvi; individual autonomy and, xx; inequalities and, xxiv; legal equality and, 68; libertarianism and, 45; National Public Radio and, xxi; nature and, 58; philosophical difficulties with, xv; political and moral crusade for, xviii; problems with underlying assumptions of, xvi; radical aims of, xii–xiii; Rawls, John approach to, xv–xvii; rights and, 44, 59, 79; social circumstances and, xvi; sociopolitical questions of, 62–65; spectrum of, 62; theories of, xiv, 73; Unger, Peter and, xviii; wealth and, 58–59. *See also* equality

"Egalitarianism an the Equal Consideration of Interests," *Concepts in Social and Political Philosophy* (Benn), 73*n*41

"Egalitarianism and Responsibility," *Journal of Ethics* 3, 62*n*3

"Egalitarianism and the Equal Consideration of Interests" (Benn), 75*n*47

"Egalitarianism *versus* Utilitarianism," *Utilitas* (Binmore), 63*n*4

Emasculating of the American Mind: How Feminism Has Enabled Mediocrity, The (Klein), 64*n*10

English Civil War, 8

Enlightenment, 17

Enlightenment Project, 21, 29; atheism and, 12; axiological element and, 13; axiological problem for, 16; countercurrent to, 22–23; denial of self and, 16–17; difficulties of, 21–22; endorsement of liberal culture and, 17–18; epistemological element of, 13, 14; Hume, David on, 21–22; influential philosophers of, 11; metaphysical element of, 13, 14, 16; origin of, 11–12; original intent of, 17; philosophical elements of, 13; philosophies of, 11; psychology and, 15, 16; Randall, J. H. and, 12; rejection of status quo and, 15; theism and, 15; transformation of rights conception, 20–21; Voltaire and, 12

Enlightenment Project in the Analytic Conversation, The (Capaldi), 11*n*6

Enquiry Concerning the Principles of Morals (Hume), 21

environmental determinism, 14

"Environmental Egalitarianism and 'Who do you Save?'" *Environmental Values* 6 (Michael), 62*n*3

equal opportunity, 52; distributive justice and, 53; duty to extend, 54;

PHILOSOPHIC REFLECTIONS

ON A FREE SOCIETY

A Series Edited by Tibor R. Machan

Business Ethics in the Global Market

Education in a Free Society

Morality and Work

*Individual Rights Reconsidered: Are the Truths of
the U.S. Declaration of Independence Lasting?*

The Commons: Its Tragedies and Other Follies

Liberty and Equality

Liberty and Hard Cases